Contents

Acknowledgements

The authors would like to thank the following organisations and individuals for their assistance and advice.

The Joseph Rowntree Foundation, who supported the study.

The Research Advisory Group, for their commitment, for their invaluable contribution to the research at every stage, and especially for their ability to both support us as individuals and to offer critical and constructive comments, while leaving us free to come to our own conclusions. They are not in any way responsible for the views expressed in the report, but it would have been all the poorer without them. The group members were as follows:

Barbara Ballard (Joseph Rowntree Foundation)
Olwen Edwards (Nottinghamshire Inter-Agency Domestic Violence Forum)
Joan Evans (Enfield Women's Aid)
Jane Geraghty (South Yorkshire Probation Service)
Nicola Harwin (Women's Aid Federation [England])
Rebecca Morley (University of Nottingham)
Audrey Mullender (University of Warwick)
Lorna Smith (Home Office)
Andrea Tara-Chand (Leeds Inter-Agency Project)
Monica Townsend (Crown Prosecution Service)
Annette Young (Department of Health)

We would also like to thank The Policy Press, and Dawn Louise Pudney in particular for all her editing work and support.

Many officers from voluntary and statutory organisations participated in the research, both in the initial mapping study and in the research carried out in the study areas. Members of domestic violence forums in these areas were actively involved in the study. A variety of individuals commented on drafts of material, including, in particular, Gill Roberts from Welsh Women's Aid and Davina James-Hanman from London Borough of Islington Women's Equality Unit. We are most grateful for all the time and the information and other help which they gave.

We are also indebted to representatives from some of the more established inter-agency initiatives which were not included as study areas. Without the work of many of them and of the Women's Aid federations and women's refuges, inter-agency work on domestic violence would be very much less advanced.

We wish to give very special thanks to the women we interviewed who had experienced domestic violence and who were prepared to discuss their views with us. We deeply value their generosity in giving us their time and attention at a time of crisis in their lives when it must have been far from easy to do so.

We also owe special thanks to Valerie Douglas for all her work and her help in meeting tight deadlines during the drafting and redrafting of this report. It could not have been done without her.

Lastly, perhaps, we can acknowledge to one another as a team our sense of achievement on completing the project. We all hope that, in some small ways at least, our work will contribute to developing policies and practices that will repay all the help and support we have had from so many individuals and organisations.

Summary

This report describes a national two-year research study of the development of inter-agency initiatives as a response to domestic violence, conducted between 1994 and 1996, and supported by the Joseph Rowntree Foundation.

Part I: The context of inter-agency work, the study and the study areas

Chapter 1: Introduction

1. Inter-agency work on domestic violence is not new. It began at least as far back as the 1970s when the newly set up Women's Aid groups began working to ensure support from relevant statutory agencies for women and their children escaping domestic violence.

2. Multi-agency initiatives began to emerge in the 1980s, often starting at local authority level.

3. Encouragement of such initiatives at national level has developed from the second half of the 1980s onwards, with Home Office circulars, a series of reports from a number of commissions and working groups, the House of Commons Home Affairs Committee Inquiry and the *Government reply* to this Inquiry. Following the setting up of the Inter-departmental Ministerial and Officials Groups on Domestic Violence by the government, the Home Office issued an Inter-agency Circular (Home Office, 1995) to stimulate the further development of coordinated inter-agency work at a local level.

Chapter 2: Background literature

4. A body of literature exists which discusses the issues involved in multi-agency work in a number of fields: looking at both the difficulties and the benefits of the multi-agency approach; at different models for coordinated agency responses; and analysing some of the conceptual, policy and practice issues.

5. There is also a specific literature about, and documentation of, multi-agency work on domestic violence both in Britain and in other countries, where attempts have been made to develop coordinated multi-faceted responses.

Chapter 3: The study

6. The aim of this national study was to investigate and to analyse inter-agency responses to domestic violence across the country in order to provide policy and practice discussion and guidance and to facilitate the further development of the inter-agency approach.

7. The research was conducted in two stages:

■ a **mapping study**, conducted during 1994 and 1995, in which all local authority areas were surveyed;

- an **in-depth study** in 1995 and 1996 of three localities and **policy and practice profile studies** in five further areas.

8. The study areas were chosen to include a spread of geographical localities with varying demographic and socio-economic characteristics. Rural as well as urban areas were included as well as areas with varying ethnic populations.

Chapter 4: Initiatives in the study areas

9. Initiatives in the study areas had a variety of origins, and took differing forms, influenced by local factors, as well as by national policy and international policy and practice. These factors include:

- existing relationships between agencies and existing networks;

- the strength or otherwise of women's community group activities, including Women's Aid groups and other refuges, advocacy and support services, groups for black women and women from different minority ethnic communities etc;

- the nature of the local community itself;

- the degree of activity of the police, probation, the local authority and other statutory agencies in inter-agency work.

Part II: Issues in multi-agency work

Chapter 5: Setting up and getting established

10. No easily distinguishable models of inter-agency domestic violence work were revealed during the study.

11. Though many similarities existed between initiatives in different localities, there was wide variation in:

- the geographic area covered;

- who took the initial initiative;

- the spread of agencies represented;

- the level of seniority of representatives;

- how initiatives were structured;

- how differences in power between agencies were approached/resolved;

- how differences in philosophy and ethos were resolved/dealt with;

- working practices;

- the type of work done;

- the type and level of any resources or funding;

- how any workers were employed etc.

12. Local conditions and circumstances determined how and whether an initiative developed. Personalities could be important. Historical, demographic, political and geographic factors which influence local developments included:

- the presence or absence of refuges and specialist domestic violence projects and the history of such development;

- the commitment of local statutory agencies including the local authority and its departments;

- the strategy of the local police force in regard to setting up both domestic violence forums and also police domestic violence units;

- the availability of resources;

- the degree of activity of local women's groups and networks;

- the presence or absence of specialist local authority units such as women's equality or community safety units;

- the political complexion of the local authority;

- the degree of agency commitment at senior management level;

- the personalities, commitments and work priorities of local personnel.

Chapter 6: Structure and organisational issues

13. Informal liaison, networking and co-ordination of services which may have developed between local agencies, including refuges, over many years, or inter-agency liaison on specific projects (eg, setting up a multi-agency training course) could be as effective as more formal liaison.

14. 'Formal' projects often took the form of a 'domestic violence forum' bringing together all or most of the relevant agencies in order to work toward coordinating services. More than 200 local forums were identified.

15. Agencies most commonly represented in inter-agency forums were:

■ Women's Aid and other local women's refuges and advocacy services;

■ the police;

■ local authority specialist units;

■ social services departments;

■ housing departments;

■ probation;

■ Victim Support;

■ other voluntary sector organisations;

■ other women's and community organ-isations;

■ health service professionals;

■ solicitors.

16. However, social services, housing departments and health service profes-sionals were less involved than expected from the potential importance of their role, while education departments rarely participated.

17. More formalised initiatives have developed written documentation, includ-ing *guiding principles* and *aims and objectives*.

These may have led, in turn, to more fully developed *terms of reference*, including *equal opportunity policies*, *mission statements*, *procedural guidelines* etc.

18. Forums developed organisational structures of various types, for example:

■ one inclusive forum meeting at greater or lesser intervals;

■ often combined with a steering committee/management committee;

■ and with sub-groups undertaking particular activities.

19. Forums varied as to their structural situation within either the statutory or the voluntary sector:

■ some were 'hosted' by a statutory agency;

■ some were situated within the voluntary sector;

■ they differed in terms of structural formality (eg what type of constitution they had, if any);

■ they differed as to whether they were incorporated or had charitable status etc.

20. Initiatives varied as to whether or not they employed any workers and if so, how they were managed. The employment of coordinators or development workers in general had a transforming effect on the work and achievements of a forum.

21. The resources available to initiatives also varied greatly:

■ an ad hoc, piecemeal approach to resourcing led to difficulties in planning and in project development;

■ most initiatives had no resourcing at all beyond what member agencies could donate or share;

■ lack of resources was the single greatest difficulty experienced by inter-agency projects.

22. Current best practice by initiatives was to avoid competing with Women's Aid, the refuge movement, and other emergency services for women and children, in seeking resourcing.

23. On the contrary, best practice was for domestic violence forums actively to

facilitate funding and other resourcing for the development of these services.

24. The level of seniority of representatives was an important issue. Respondents discussed:

■ the need for a mixture of policy makers and grass-roots organisations and practitioners in the initiative;

■ where forum members were mainly practitioners, the need to develop links and regular meetings with senior managers and policy makers to carry policy innovations forward;

■ the importance of the full involvement of the voluntary sector, especially refuge-based women's advocacy services;

■ the need for representatives from statutory agencies to be at a senior enough level to be able to influence that agency or to be given a status which allowed them to liaise with policy makers within their agency.

25. In some areas strategy-making inter-agency bodies, at a level wider than the basic unitary authority and consisting of senior policy-making officers from each agency, were thought to be an advantage, although such groups have had mixed success so far.

26. It was also thought to be important to have consistency of attendance and active commitment from members and for agencies to delegate representatives to participate in the forum, steering committee, or sub-group, as part of their job descriptions.

27. Respondents also pointed out the value of having strategies in place within the initiative to deal with disagreements and differences in power between agencies, and to counteract the tendency of statutory agencies to 'take over' the initiative.

28. One of the difficulties faced was that of developing a coherent working philosophy on domestic violence and avoiding a 'lowest common denominator' effect.

Chapter 7: Work done by inter-agency initiatives

29. Types of work done included:

■ networking;

■ agency coordination (eg, producing resource directories);

■ domestic violence training (often delivered on a 'Training the Trainers' basis);

■ policy and practice guidance developed with individual agencies or on a multi-agency basis;

■ preventative work (eg, improved refuge, advocacy and advice/helpline provision; perpetrators projects, etc);

■ public education work (including Zero Tolerance campaigns and other awareness-raising activities, producing information material for abused women and children, etc);

■ other educational work (eg, producing education packs for use in schools and in youth work);

■ setting up new projects (eg, women's support groups and advice services);

■ conducting research, monitoring developments, collecting local statistics, acting in an advisory capacity and as a 'watchdog' on the quality of local services, etc.

Chapter 8: The participation of the statutory sector, Victim Support and national voluntary organisations

The police

30. Much useful inter-agency domestic violence work has been done by the police resulting from Home Office and police initiatives. There was evidence that police-initiated projects work best where the police refrain from taking too much of a dominant role (eg, avoiding habitually taking the chair at meetings, recognising

the problems involved in holding forum meetings on police station premises etc). There was also evidence of initiatives working better where dedicated domestic violence officer posts or a local domestic violence unit existed.

31. The police were sometimes involved at policy-making level, with commitment from senior management, and with developed practice and policy guidance and training programmes.

32. However, interviews suggested that a number of agencies and grass-roots organisations had doubts about the extent and depth of change in recent domestic violence policing. Doubts were also expressed about the social control function of the police, its masculine ethos and the existence of aggressive and potentially racist policing practice in relation to certain groups. These issues could result in difficulties in inter-agency cooperation.

Probation

33. The probation service took a role in some inter-agency initiatives, often through involvement with perpetrators groups. The study found that individual probation officers frequently attended domestic violence forums and in some areas senior probation officers were involved in joint multi-agency groups with police and other senior policy makers to evolve a coordinated local domestic violence strategy. Probation services in various areas had developed, or were developing, new practice guidelines on domestic violence. In other cases, if it occurred at all, involvement of the probation service in domestic violence forums might occur almost in spite of, rather than because of the agency, with a lack of participation or commitment from managers. Further local and national guidance on this issue would be useful.

Other areas of the justice system

34. The Crown Prosecution Service, judges and magistrates, and other court personnel from both the civil and criminal justice systems were rarely involved in inter-agency domestic violence initiatives. However, a few domestic violence forums had developed training packages for magistrates and court officers and had initiated projects to support abused women using the court system. Private solicitors firms were more often active in local domestic violence forums and in some cases took a leading role.

The local authority

35. Social services were less well represented in multi-agency initiatives than may have been expected in view of their key responsibility for services to children and families. As for other agencies, forums were often attended by basic grade social workers on an ad hoc basis or out of personal interest. Although area team managers were involved in some of the main study areas this was relatively rare. Participants in the study expressed their disappointment at this situation and pointed out the need for the commitment of senior management. When a departmental policy commitment did exist social workers were able to take a more active role for the mutual benefit of the forum and the department.

36. Such a lack of active commitment may reflect pressures on social workers' time, or a lack of priority accorded to domestic violence within many social services teams despite some recent improvements. However, there has been a growing recognition of the connections between child abuse and domestic violence in recent years and also of the effects on children of witnessing domestic violence, which has led to greater participation of social work departments in inter-agency forums, particularly in children's work. Domestic violence also features in many community care plans, often with the involvement of multi-agency task groups, and some social services departments have developed domestic violence policies and good practice guidance. Inter-agency approaches

have been highlighted by two recent Department of Health/Social Services Inspectorate seminars and the findings of the study indicate that further national and local guidance on participation in multi-agency work would be welcome.

37. Local authority housing departments and housing associations, though they participated in a significant number of forums, were not as actively involved in multi-agency initiatives as expected, given their importance, and, in the case of housing departments, their statutory responsibility in providing the possiblity of safe affordable housing to women. Most commonly, housing departments were represented through their homelessness section or unit, usually through housing officers, but sometimes through active participation of housing managers and in some cases working with multi-agency groups to develop domestic violence policy and practice on housing issues.

38. Though they were rarely represented, some local authority education departments worked with inter-agency forums or multi-agency groups on education packs and domestic violence training.

39. Specialist local authority units such as community safety or equality units, where they existed, very often played a valuable initiating, servicing and supportive role.

Health services

40. There was poor representation in general from health care providers and purchasers. It is vital that better representation be encouraged since health services are a key link in the chain of possible protective and preventive services for women who experience domestic violence and their children. Concern was expressed at this absence, and the importance of improving the extent and level of participation by health services in multi-agency domestic violence work was stressed. National and local guidance on

this issue is required urgently and would be welcomed.

Victim Support

41. Victim Support was often an active and valuable participant in multi-agency work, and had taken a pro-active role in its development nationally. In some cases Victim Support had initiated the forum or was a key participant.

National voluntary organisations

42. As national organisations, the Women's Aid federations played a major role in the development and encouragement of multi-agency initiatives nationally.

43. Some other long-established national voluntary organisations, such as Relate and NSPCC, participated in a number of initiatives at a local level.

Chapter 9: The voluntary sector, Women's Aid and equality issues

44. The research highlighted the importance of recognising the central role of Women's Aid and independent women's refuge and advocacy services, and of avoiding both the marginalisation or isolation of the refuge movement, grass-roots women's projects and community groups, or the dilution of their philosophy.

45. Some initiatives had developed strategies to avoid these difficulties; for example, Women's Aid or local refuges took a position of power or influence (eg, on the management of the project) as a matter of agreed policy; Women's Aid chaired the forum etc. Active support from other agencies for Women's Aid and other refuge-based advocacy services parti-cipating in inter-agency initiatives was also helpful.

46. The study found that there may be a need for the national Women's Aid

federations and for other women's refuges to further develop policy and strategies about prioritising inter-agency work and about how this can be done.

47. Initiatives also need to be aware of the necessity to avoid the marginalisation of black women's projects, disabled women's projects, children's organisations, grass-roots campaigning bodies, and other community organisations.

48. Equalities issues, despite considerable progress in some areas, remained difficult and sometimes personally painful. Some initiatives had adopted a range of measures to address these questions, including equal opportunities policies and equalities training, equalities selection and recruit-ment procedures; full representation of all groups at both forum and steering committee level; the provision of support or of consultants for representatives from minority groups or communities; the setting up of equality sub-groups of forum members; and the setting up of wider equality advisory groups to monitor and advise on the work of the forum.

49. Only 5 of the 70 women survivors of domestic violence who were interviewed during the study had heard of the inter-agency initiative in their area, even in passing, but 60 out of the 70 thought that abused women should have some sort of input into multi-agency work. A number of women suggested ways in which forums could go about involving abused women and made valuable comments on service provision in the locality.

50. Some initiatives are beginning to develop ways of directly involving women and children who have experienced domestic violence. These include strategies for refuges to take a more active role as an agreed principle of their operation in terms of liaison between inter-agency initiatives and abused women and children. A newly developing and innovative practive is the setting up of survivors advisory groups or monitoring groups to informally advise on the work of the forum.

Part III: Conclusions and suggestions for future development

Chapter 10: Conclusions and key issues

51. Although innovative coordinating, preventative and educational work had been undertaken in many areas, in some there were suggestions that multi-agency work might use up resources and energy, diverting scarce funds and attention away from the provision of refuges and emergency services, and achieve little.

52. Although the issues are complex some of the factors which seemed to lead to effective action were:

■ Active involvement of the key statutory agencies at both policy-making and practitioner level, with senior man-agement support.

■ The full participation of Women's Aid and local refuge services, and the use of concrete strategies to promote their central involvement.

■ Active participation of community and grass-roots women's organisations and of the voluntary sector, at both practitioner and management level.

■ Consistent, committed attendance and membership, with members attending as agreed representatives of their agencies, where possible.

■ The adoption of *guiding principles* and common agreements about domestic violence.

■ Clear *aims and objectives, equal opportunities policies* and other *terms of reference*, regularly reviewed.

■ A clear workable structure and lines of accountability, but avoiding bureaucracy;

possibly with a representative steering committee and sub-groups.

■ Resources for activities, for co-ordination and for servicing of the forum and where possible for a coordinator or development worker with administrative support.

■ Relating all activities to the needs and safety of abused women and to decreasing domestic violence.

■ The development of concrete activities within the forum's capabilities.

■ The integration of equalities issues into all work.

■ The involvement of, and informal accountability to, women survivors of domestic violence and their children.

■ The use of evaluation and monitoring processes in specific relation to work done and its effectiveness.

53. Some concern was expressed that inter-agency work at a time of resource cut-back could act as a smoke-screen to disguise inaction, and as a face-saver for central and local government. It was pointed out that increased coordination is of little use if the resources and services needed are not in place.

54. However, most interviewees hoped that inter-agency initiatives would be an important and creative next step in moving on beyond fragmented service provision to service coordination and to preventative, educational and awareness-raising approaches.

55. To promote the latter possibility and as the next stage after the issuing of the 1995 Inter-agency Circular by the Home Office:

■ Specific guidance is needed from government departments and services other than the Home Office on the priority to be given by the full range of relevant agencies to inter-agency work on domestic violence, in order to facilitate its development as a co-ordinated multi-faceted local and national strategy.

■ To ensure adequate representation of agency staff on multi-agency initiatives, this could include guidance on building multi-agency work into job specifications for some staff and a commitment to the work at senior management and policy-making level.

■ It would also be helpful to have further development of national strategy and informal guidance for individual refuge groups by the national Women's Aid federations on the involvement of refuge-based support and advocacy services in inter-agency work.

■ Adequate resourcing is needed to facilitate the development of inter-agency work and to avoid competition for funding and resources with refuges and other direct services.

■ In view of the concern expressed by some interviewees about the statutory as well as the financial limitations on their ability to provide effective support for the aims enunciated in the Inter-agency Circular, it would be valuable for the Inter-departmental Groups, especially at ministerial level, to discuss the content of proposed legislation from the viewpoint of its impact on the provision of effective services to improve the safety of abused women as well as on the prevention of domestic violence.

56. Two of the major conclusions from this study are that: **further national and local guidance and adequate resourcing for both inter-agency domestic violence work and for refuges and other direct services are essential if the approach is to be successful.**

57. The research showed the existing potential for multi-agency work, given the right conditions, to develop further as a creative, exciting way forward in:

■ building awareness about domestic violence and its consequences;

■ creating and coordinating effective and far-reaching services;

■ helping to create a society which no longer condones such violence or minimises its impact.

Part I

The context of inter-agency work, the study and the study areas

Chapter 1

Introduction: inter-agency work and domestic violence

This report describes a national two-year research study of the development of inter-agency initiatives as a response to domestic violence, supported by the Joseph Rowntree Foundation.

Context and beginnings

In the 19th century, domestic violence was a subject of concern, of campaigning activity and of new legislation in Britain, the United States and elsewhere. However, this concern waned in the first part of the 20th century. After a long silence, violence against women in their own homes from their partners or from former partners again became a social issue in the early 1970s (Pizzey, 1974; Dobash and Dobash, 1980), when women who experienced domestic violence and their children began coming for help to women's centres set up by women's liberation groups. It quickly became obvious that this was an issue which cut across the responsibilities of local and national statutory agencies.

From the beginning it was clear that women in such a situation were not the direct concern of any particular agency. For example, they were not the responsibility of social services departments because these departments saw their brief as directed towards the welfare of children in the family, which often, at the time, implied working with 'dysfunctional' or problem families to keep them together (Maynard, 1985). They would not be considered homeless by local authority housing departments prior to the homelessness legislation of 1977, because they were considered to have a home with their husband or partner (Rose, 1985; Binney, Harkell and Nixon, 1981; 1985; Malos and Hague, 1993). If they went to the police for help, even sometimes when there had been severe and repeated violence, the assault was frequently seen as a minor incident, a 'domestic', where often the best that would happen would be that the man might be taken for a walk around the block to 'cool off' (Dunhill, 1989; Edwards, 1989). At worst, the woman herself might be treated as if she was wasting police time, or as if she herself was the offender, a situation which Mama (1989) documents, particularly in relation to black women, and which has by no means disappeared, especially where issues involving immigration or asylum might be at stake.

Inter-agency work between refuges, the Women's Aid federations (which have co-ordinated the provision of refuges and advocacy for more than 20 years), and other agencies with the potential to provide services for women experiencing domestic violence and their children, began as far back as the mid-1970s, as the new Women's Aid movement became aware of the problems that women encountered in seeking to gain access to these services.

As Women's Aid groups developed, and attempted to obtain emergency accommodation, advice and support for survivors of domestic violence and their children, they were therefore immediately faced with the imperative for inter-agency working. This could be inter-agency work in its narrower sense of negotiating with individual statutory agencies at the local level to get a property for a refuge, or attempting to ensure that the needs of women coming to the refuge would be recognised and met. Such inter-agency liaison could be one-off, intermittent, or more or less continuous. Sometimes inter-agency work involved working with individuals or representatives of voluntary organisations and statutory agencies to lobby for funding for refuges and other similar services, or to challenge poor policy and bad practice on the part of statutory agencies, like the (then) Department of Health and Social Security, local authority housing departments, social services departments or the police (Binney, Harkell and Nixon, 1981; Pahl, 1985; Dobash and Dobash, 1992).

At other times, this effort was directed towards changing policy at a more fundamental level. This can be seen in the inter-agency work which gave rise to the 1976 Domestic Violence and Matrimonial Proceedings Act and the 1978 Domestic Violence and Magistrates Courts Act, extending and modifying the use of civil protection orders in cases of domestic violence. At the time of writing, these laws are in the process of being replaced by the relevant clauses of the 1996 Family Law Act in response to criticisms of their shortcoming in practice (Barron, 1990; Law Commission, 1992). Similarly, it was a multi-agency alliance with housing organisations, members of parliament, and others, which brought the recognition, in the 1977 Housing (Homeless Persons) Act, that women and others who were unable to live in the family home because of violence or the threat of violence were, in fact, homeless and that it was the duty of local authority housing departments to secure

accommodation for them (Malos, 1993; Malos and Hague, 1993). This duty will soon be curtailed by the new 1996 Housing Act.

Official encouragement for inter-agency work on domestic violence

It was from a growing awareness of the shortcomings of a piecemeal approach in which each service and agency treated each 'case' in isolation, and from a parallel awareness of developing multi-agency work in a few localities, that more coordinated official efforts towards setting up inter-agency initiatives began to emerge in the 1980s. These often started at the local authority level, partially arising from the funding of some refuges or refuge services by housing or social services departments, and further developed later on with the establishment of local authority women's units, equality units or community safety units. In 1990, the Convention of Scottish Local Authorities convened a Women and Violence Working Group, with representation from Scottish Women's Aid, as well as officers and elected members of Scottish local authorities. The Working Group's report of 1991 recognised the importance of refuges and direct support services for women and advocated the development of multi-agency cooperation as a matter of urgency (Hague and Malos, 1993). In England, pioneering inter-agency initiatives developed in the late 1980s in various areas, for example, Nottinghamshire, Wolverhampton, Hammersmith and Fulham and Leeds (Hague and Malos, 1993). The more general development of multi-agency initiatives on domestic violence owes much to their example.

The encouragement of such initiatives at the level of national policy followed a somewhat different path. Throughout the 1980s, there were increasing concerns expressed about violence against women – especially about rape and domestic violence – in all sections of the media.

These were partly prompted by the women's movement and by a number of well publicised cases. In addition, an increasing number of academic studies were becoming available (for example, Dobash and Dobash, 1980; Binney, 1981; Hanmer and Saunders, 1984; Edwards, 1986) which in turn fuelled growing interest in the subject. An influential report by the Women's National Commission (1985), an advisory body to the government, called for more serious and considerate treatment of women who had experienced both rape and domestic violence.

The Home Office (1986) responded by issuing a Circular to all Chief Officers of Police (69/86), advising that the over-riding concern in respect of domestic violence was to ensure the safety of victims and to reduce the risk of further violence. The Circular also suggested that consideration should be given to ensuring that information be provided on the sources of assistance and support available for women experiencing domestic violence. In addition, the Home Office set in train a wide-ranging critical review of the research literature on all aspects of domestic violence which would inform policy making across government. This report (Smith, 1989) led to a further Circular to the police (60/90) from the Home Office (1990) which, among other things, advocated inter-agency liaison. It was also referred to the Ministerial Group on Women's Issues (which at that point was chaired by John Patten, then Minister of State at the Home Office) in order to stimulate action across all government departments.

As discussed in Chapter 2, a further impetus was added by the National Inter-Agency Working Party convened by Victim Support and involving a number of statutory and voluntary agencies, including the Women's Aid Federation (England), which reported in 1992 (National Inter-Agency Working Party, 1992). The House of Commons Home Affairs Committee *Inquiry into domestic violence* (1993), with the published *Government reply* (1993), provided the next main development in policy making at a national level. It may also be relevant that the British government had signed the United Nations Convention on the Elimination of all Forms of Discrimination Against Women, augmented by a Declaration on the Elimination of Violence Against Women (United Nations, 1990; 1993). The signing of such conventions and declarations places an obligation on signatory governments to report on action taken to implement their provisions.

Following the Home Affairs Committee Report, Inter-departmental Ministerial and Officials Groups on Domestic Violence were set up, convened by the Home Office, which has been identified as the lead government department in coordinating domestic violence policy. The work of these committees led to the issuing of the government Inter-agency Circular, *Inter-agency coordination to tackle domestic violence*, in 1995 (Home Office, 1995).

The advice in the Inter-agency Circular concentrates on the desirability of inter-agency work in the local setting. As will be seen from the discussion of inter-agency initiatives in the research areas in Part II, Home Office Crime Prevention and Safer Cities projects have given further encouragement to developments in some areas (see Morley and Mullender, 1994, for an assessment of one such project and an overview of the general issues). Various partnership initiatives have added a further element. Multi-agency domestic violence work has been the subject of consultations between a variety of agencies and the Women's Aid federations, which have provided training and support to many inter-agency initiatives in the last few years.

The research described in this report is a study of such local coordination of services and of resulting policy and practice development. However, the brief review of the historical context of inter-agency working presented above indicates that effective practice at the local level depends to a significant extent on national legislation and national policies. A number of those interviewed during the preparation for this research project expressed the view that local inter-agency cooperation needs to be backed up at regional or national level.

The original initiative for the research study, which has been generously supported by the Joseph Rowntree Foundation, came from the Women's Aid federations, in particular the Women's Aid Federation (England) (WAFE); from various inter-agency domestic violence projects; and from a variety of statutory and voluntary organisations and agencies. The study was developed as a wide-ranging investigation of inter-agency approaches to domestic violence as a policy and practice option.

While the term 'inter-agency' is widely used in domestic violence circles, the term 'multi-agency' more properly explains the type of cooperation between agencies which is current in domestic violence work and which is described in this research study. Therefore, 'inter-agency' and 'multi-agency' are used interchangeably throughout this report. Inter-agency initiatives frequently take the form of local domestic violence forums bringing together all the relevant agencies in the locality in question.

Chapter 2

Background literature

The multi-agency approach – in general

In recent years, there has been a considerable amount of literature discussing the issues involved in multi-agency work in a number of fields. Inter-agency coordination in general has, to a limited degree, been on the social and political agenda for a number of decades, but currently enjoys wide-spread popularity and official support, particularly within community care, crime prevention, and child protection. Smith et al (1993) for example, have discussed a variety of approaches to inter-agency coordination within the health services and community care. Ideas about collaborative working have also been studied by Arblaster et al, 1996; Hudson, 1987; Webb, 1991; Goss and Kent, 1995, and many others, in relation to public sector management and social welfare policy regarding care in the community, housing and health. However, only a small section of the relevant literature can be touched on in this review.

Research studies and analysis, together with other publications about the issue (eg, policy and practice documents), demonstrate that inter-agency collaboration is a complex task, with many potential difficulties. It has been suggested that collaboration of this type may be very limited in practice or may lead to rather sporadic attempts to initiate improvements which often then peter out (Gill and Pickles, 1989). A recent project, sponsored by the Joseph Rowntree Foundation, used an action research model to study inter-agency approaches to responding to young people in difficulty in Oxford (Lloyd, 1994). In common with other such studies, this study found that local attempts to establish a wide range of inter-agency activity needed greater coordination in order to be effective (Lloyd, 1994, p 10). Difficulties to be overcome included a lack of strategic planning across agencies, conflicting legislation, financial constraints, the limits imposed on agencies by their own individual budgets, and uncertainties about the roles and responsibilities of different agencies and how these could be shared (Lloyd, 1994, pp 34-35).

Despite these difficulties, there is currently a certain enthusiasm for multi-agency and partnership approaches within both local and central government. In relation to child protection, inter-agency liaison takes a formalised, statutory form, and partnership of various types is enshrined within the 1989 Children Act (see, for example, the Department of Health [DoH] publication, *Working together: a guide to arrangements for inter-agency co-operation for the protection of children from abusers*, 1988; also Hallet, 1995). In some areas of work, government support has led to the setting up of specific multi-agency projects on a nation-wide basis. A government initiative, for example, has led to guidance on the establishment of multi-agency drug action teams and drug reference groups in local areas to deal with drug use and abuse (see Howard, Beadle and Maitland, 1993; DoH, 1994; 1995).

Within crime prevention, inter-agency work has been increasingly seen as the way forward. The theory behind this development suggests that crime prevention can only be effective if the police and the rest of the criminal justice system participate in a coordinated, multi-faceted response, involving a range of services and community involvement (Home Office Crime Prevention Unit, 1987; Liddle and Gelsthorpe, 1994a,b,c). Such multi-agency approaches to crime prevention may have a broad remit. The Five Towns Initiative, for example, used a wide-ranging inter-agency approach to demonstrate that a variety of interested local agencies working together in five separate localities could reduce crime in their local communities (Home Office Crime Prevention Unit, 1987; Liddle and Bottoms, 1994).

The inter-agency approach to crime has tended to be traditionally regarded from two conflicting perspectives. One of these is that agencies are largely benevolent and that collaboration will improve crime prevention and services offered. The other sees inter-agency coordination as potentially having social control and civil liberties implications in terms of greater surveillance of service users and others, and the possible domination of community agencies by the police in particular (Holder, forthcoming).

Work over the last few years produced by the Home Office has been useful in analysing the complexity of the issue (Liddle and Gelsthorpe, 1994a; 1994b; 1994c; Sampson et al, 1988; 1991; Sampson, 1991). Liddle and Gelsthorpe produced three reports in a series on the subject of inter-agency crime prevention addressing a wide range of issues, including a consideration of race and gender factors. In common with Sampson et al (1988; 1991) and other researchers (eg, Blagg et al, 1988), they point out that inter-agency relations are: "highly complicated, seldom static, and influenced by a variety of institutional, individual and local/historical factors." (Liddle and Gelsthorpe, 1994b, p 26).

They describe five possible models of inter-agency cooperation (Liddle and Gelsthorpe, 1994b; Gelsthorpe, 1985):

- the communication model

- the cooperation model

- the coordination model

- the federation model

- the merger model.

They also discuss the concept of a 'lead agency' and the need for inter-agency projects to have some sort of structure (Liddle and Gelsthorpe, 1994a). Different agencies adopt a variety of forms of participation in multi-agency initiatives, varying from 'prime movers' to 'sleeping partners', and the most effective style of working for inter-agency projects appears to be one which could be known as 'multi-agency problem-solving' (Liddle and Gelsthorpe, 1994b). Liddle and Gelsthorpe (1994a; 1994b) propose that strategy level crime prevention groups need to consist of higher managers, but that grass-roots level groups can be effective if they have the active support of, and effective lines of communication with, senior level staff.

Sampson continues this analysis, describing the importance of power differences and struggles between agencies, of gender and race factors, of different perceptions, analyses and understandings of the problem being addressed, and of conflicts over tasks and priorities. She and other researchers also describe the tendency of agencies to 'protect their own turf'. Sampson points out the need for a core working group with the power to make decisions (Sampson, 1991). Various research studies have found that inter-agency projects are generally poor at conducting evaluation and at monitoring their work (Home Office, 1991, p 22; Liddle and Gelsthorpe, 1994c, p 16).

Lack of resources has been the subject of research findings and of much debate in terms of its hampering effect on multi-agency coordination. Liddle and Gelsthorpe found that, while there were considerable variations in resource level for different inter-agency crime prevention projects, the lack of resources overall was frequently believed to be the largest obstacle to effective work (Liddle and Gelsthorpe, 1994c, p 14). These authors and others, writing in Home Office publications, also point out that a perceived lack of resources could serve as an excuse for inaction and that resources were sometimes wasted in duplicated effort (Liddle and Gelsthorpe, 1994c, pp 14-15; Home Office, 1991, p 26).

The multi-agency approach – domestic violence

In recent years, as discussed in Chapter 1, the inter-agency approach has become increasingly popular as a specific policy and practice response to domestic violence. With the publication of the 1995 Inter-agency Circular (Home Office, 1995), the approach has been encouraged by the government as one of the principal planks of its domestic violence policy.

This has tended to place violence against women in the home within a community safety or crime prevention context, and runs alongside recent understandings of domestic violence as a crime in its own right (Smith, 1989; Home Office, 1990; Barron, Harwin and Singh; 1992, Walker and McNichol, 1994; Grace, 1995; Cretney and Davis, 1996; Morley and Mullender, 1994). As noted in Chapter 1, the police response to domestic violence has improved substantially in recent years, particularly following the Home Office Circular 60/90 (Home Office, 1990) and related guidance. This guidance aims to encourage pro-arrest and pro-prosecution policies for offenders and to offer support to abused women and children, through the operation of dedicated domestic violence officer posts and domestic violence units. Recent research (Grace, 1995) shows that, while very real gains have been made as a result, these improvements are uneven and patchy across the country (see also Morley and Mullender, 1994; Hague and Malos,

1993, pp 65-85; Cretney and Davis, 1996; Walker and McNicol, 1994).

As noted, the Home Office guidance also recommends the setting up of multi-agency domestic violence forums by local police forces in an attempt to coordinate local responses (Home Office, 1990; Morley and Mullender, 1994; Hague and Malos, 1993). The Home Office study by Grace, cited above, which evaluated the effectiveness of domestic violence policing in the 1990s, found that relatively few police forces were actively engaged in multi-agency domestic violence work at the time that the research was conducted, but that the vast majority liaised informally with other agencies (Grace, 1995, p 6). The study suggests that police involvement in inter-agency cooperation is still in need of improvement, coordination and expansion in order to be effective, and that all forces should consider participation in the development of inter-agency forums and in joint domestic violence training (Grace, 1995, p ix).

However, expressed interest in multi-agency domestic violence work extends far beyond criminal justice and community safety arenas. The inter-agency approach to dealing with domestic violence has been widely recommended internationally by the United Nations and other bodies (for example, by the UN Expert Group on Violence in the Family, 1986, the UN Manual for Practitioners, and the 1987 European Colloquy on Violence within the Family).

The approach has also been encouraged in many different arenas and localities within Britain. Inter-agency coordination regarding domestic violence has been recommended by the National Association of Local Government Women's Committees, now Women in Local Authority Network (NALGWC, 1989, currently being updated), and by various previously cited bodies and reports, including the 1985 Women's National Commission Report, the influential 1989 Home Office paper by

Lorna Smith (Smith, 1989), the National Inter-Agency Working Party Report (1992), and the 1993 House of Commons Home Affairs Committee Inquiry (Home Affairs Committee, 1993). The WAFE evidence to this Inquiry also recommended improved inter-agency liaison (Barron, Harwin and Singh, 1992, p 1). Recommendation 41 of the Inquiry Report suggested specifically that the government encourage local multi-agency cooperation on domestic violence (Home Affairs Committee, 1993). This recommendation was supported in the *Government reply* to the Inquiry (1993, p 17) in regard to: "how inter-agency good practice, once it has been identified, can be promulgated throughout the country". A recent report (Ball, 1996) from the Social Services Inspectorate of the DoH also discusses and encourages inter-agency approaches to domestic violence.

Evidence from other countries has shown that an effective policy response to domestic violence can only occur if there is extensive coordination and agency collaboration (Morley and Mullender, 1994, p 26). In some areas of the US, a co-ordinated and multi-faceted response to domestic violence in various localities has involved collaboration between the criminal justice system, other agencies and community services and women's initiatives (Goolkasian, 1986; Cahn and Lerman, 1991; Edelson, 1991). Specific intervention projects have evolved which often have close links with the shelter (refuge) movement and are situated independently of the criminal justice services (Morley and Mullender, 1994, p 16; Pence and Shepard, 1988).

The coordinated community response developed by the Duluth Domestic Abuse Intervention Project in Minnesota has received particular attention in this country, and has led to the elaboration of the 'Duluth model' as a multi-agency response to domestic violence (Pence and Shepard, 1988; Pence, 1988; McMahon and Pence, forthcoming). This model includes extensive coordination of criminal justice system responses with daily monitoring by the Domestic Abuse Intervention Project and the development of 'community confrontation' of domestic abuse (see Pence, 1988, for a discussion of this issue); of accountability to abused women; and of training modules based on analyses of gender issues of power and control between men and women.

Inter-agency interventions in response to domestic violence have arisen elsewhere in the US and in Canada (eg, the London Coordinating Committee to end Woman Abuse in Ontario). Multi-faceted co-ordinated responses also exist at both state and federal level in New Zealand and in Australia (McGregor and Hopkins, 1991; see also Gardiner, forthcoming). The research team has collected evidence that some multi-agency domestic violence initiatives have been, or are being, established in various other countries around the world. A few examples, among many, include India, Zimbabwe, South Africa, and a number of European countries, for instance, France, Holland, and Sweden.

In this country, the potential strengths and weaknesses of the inter-agency response to domestic violence have been discussed in a wide variety of conferences and in a number of publications, some initiated by the Women's Aid federations or by Women's Aid refuges (Dublin Women's Aid, 1995; Convention of Scottish Local Authorities, 1991). These have sometimes echoed the issues brought up by Liddle and Gelsthorpe and by Sampson, but in the context of the refuge network and the women's movement against domestic violence.

The role of refuges and of other services for women and children experiencing domestic violence within inter-agency initiatives has been an issue of debate in these discussions and publications (Hague and Malos, 1993, pp 185-87; National Inter-Agency Working Party, 1992). The need for a coordinated national policy on the provision of refuges and other services for abused women and children has been often stated (Barron, Harwin and Singh, 1992;

Home Affairs Committee, 1993; Hague and Malos, 1993, pp 166-74), although there are concerns that this may be overlooked in the move towards inter-agency cooperation. Hague and Malos (1993, pp 178-91) discuss how inter-agency work on domestic violence can act, on the one hand, as a constructive way forward and, on the other, as a 'face-saving' development which may disguise inaction and lack of commitment.

Issues of racism and other types of discrimination have a particular resonance in regard to inter-agency work on domestic violence. Mama (1989, pp 92-138 and p 314) discusses these issues. She points out that multi-agency responses are important and worthwhile, but that it is imperative that these responses should not multiply the suffering which abused black women and children endure, but should rather alleviate it (Mama, 1989, p 92). Mama presents evidence, based within a historical overview of the situation of black women in Britain, that it is the former, and not the latter, which happens in many instances. Southall Black Sisters have put forward a view that the involvement of police forces in inter-agency work can cause tensions and difficulties for some other groups, that the police sometimes use the multi-agency

project for their own ends, and that liaison with the police may be inappropriate in such circumstances due to examples of oppressive or racist policing practices in black or minority ethnic communities (Southall Black Sisters, 1989; Patel, forthcoming). The literature indicates that these issues have yet to be resolved.

Various inter-agency projects have, themselves, conducted research (see, for example, Dominy and Radford, 1996), and some have conducted specific projects. The London Borough of Islington Women's Equality Unit and the Islington Inter-agency Domestic Violence Working Party, for example, have produced reports on the needs of disabled women, and of black women and women from minority ethnic communities, who are experiencing domestic violence (see, for example, London Borough of Islington, 1995a). Lastly, a 1995 working paper on inter-agency initiates as a response to domestic violence discusses both the strengths and the possible pitfalls of such initiatives as a result of the first stage of this research study (Hague, Malos and Dear, 1995a). The findings of the research in full are presented in the rest of this report.

Chapter 3

The study

This national research study aimed to investigate, describe and analyse inter-agency responses to domestic violence across the country. When the study commenced, many multi-agency domestic violence initiatives were, to a greater or lesser extent, in a position of having 'to re-invent the wheel' because they were not always aware of the work of other more established multi-agency bodies. The aims of the study were, therefore, to provide policy and practice discussion and guidance in order to facilitate the further development of the inter-agency approach.

In the study, domestic violence inter-agency work was described and analysed according to a number of factors, including the participation of both statutory and voluntary sector agencies; the impact of the initiating agency; structure and working practices; the availability of resources; the activities engaged in and their effectiveness; power differences between agencies and decision making; the role of Women's Aid and the refuge movement; equalities issues; and the views and participation of women who had experienced domestic violence.

Overall methodology

The methods used in this study are described in detail in Appendix A.

The research was conducted in two stages:

i) **A mapping study** of inter-agency domestic violence initiatives in England, Scotland and Wales. All local authority areas were investigated through a national telephone survey, supplemented by face-to-face interviews where appropriate, and the collection of documents and literature.

ii) **An in-depth study** of three local areas, and **policy and practice profile studies** in five further areas. In the three main study areas, interviews were carried out with a wide range of local agencies and with a sample of women who had experienced domestic violence. In the policy and practice profile study areas, interviews were conducted with a variety of organisations, but not with abused women. In all eight areas, interview methods were supplemented by observation, attendance at meetings, and the analysis of documentation, of publications and of policy and practice guidance produced. These studies were further supplemented by secondary research in, and by some interviews with, the best-known inter-agency initiatives not otherwise investigated in the research (eg, the Leeds Inter-agency Project, the London Borough of Islington Inter-agency Domestic Violence Working Party and the London Borough of Hammersmith and Fulham Domestic Violence Forum).

The research areas were chosen according to the criteria listed in Appendix A, pp 88-91. The three localities which were selected as main study areas for the research project were **Derby**, **Walsall** and

Cleveland. The five policy and practice profile study areas selected were **South Yorkshire**, **North Wales**, **Bristol**, **Dorset** and the **London Borough of Greenwich**.

The main study areas

Choice of areas

■ Derby was chosen as one of the main study areas due to the progress of work in the city on domestic violence. Derby is a small city with a sizeable population of various minority ethnic communities. It has active anti-racist, feminist and disability movements. The Derby Domestic Violence Action Group (henceforth referred to as DDVAG) was established in 1991.

■ During the mapping study, Derby was clearly identified as an area where a great deal of inter-agency domestic violence work was being conducted and specialist workers had been employed. Unlike many inter-agency domestic violence forums, the Derby project had developed a working structure and *terms of reference*, and had begun to take on issues of equality of opportunity as an integral part of the work done. One of the research remits was to address these types of issues. Another was to look at the involvement of Women's Aid and the refuge movement in inter-agency initiatives. The initial work indicated that Women's Aid was well-represented in the Derby project through the active participation of the Hadhari Nari Project, which operates the Women's Aid refuges in the city, and offers support to all women and children, but to black women and children in particular. Other refuges were also closely involved. The research team felt, therefore, that DDVAG fulfilled the research criteria in these respects. In addition, DDVAG had received less publicity at the time that the research began than some long-established projects, for example, the Leeds Inter-agency Project.

■ Cleveland was also chosen as one of the main study areas due to the wide extent of work in the county on domestic violence. The Cleveland Domestic Violence Multi-agency Forum was established in 1991. Women's Aid has been an active participant throughout, and various initiatives were set into place in the first few years. There are several refuges in the Cleveland area, including an Asian women's refuge, which was in existence for half of the study period.

■ The employment of paid coordinators for the multi-agency domestic violence initiative and for a Zero Tolerance campaign in Cleveland, and the wide geographical area covered by the initiative, were factors which were investigated during the mapping study and which contributed to the inclusion of Cleveland in the study. The area covered by the previous county of Cleveland, which was replaced by four unitary authorities in April 1996, includes small towns, rural areas, and a large urban conurbation. It contains a variety of types of community. While there are Asian and smaller African Caribbean communities in Middlesbrough and the other towns, the population as a whole is mainly white.

■ Cleveland was clearly identified as an area where innovative inter-agency domestic violence work was being conducted which complemented and differed from the work in Derby and Walsall. Unlike the Derby project, the Cleveland project was not constituted as a voluntary sector project, but rather was 'hosted' by the local authority social services department. The project had begun to attempt to take on issues of equality of opportunity. Another factor in the choice of Cleveland as a main study area was the central role played by Women's Aid and the refuge movement in the inter-agency initiative. In addition, as for Derby and Walsall, Cleveland had received less publicity at the time that the research was commenced than some other long-established projects.

■ Other research criteria were that study areas should provide a wide geographical spread across the country. The research team particularly wished to avoid the over-emphasis on London and on the southern areas of the country which can be identified in some research projects. For this reason, the team were pleased to be able to work in Cleveland.

■ Walsall was selected to be part of the research study because the domestic violence forum there had initially been established by the police, in common with many forums throughout the West Midlands. The Walsall Domestic Violence Forum had existed for several years and had been actively facilitated by the local police force. It therefore provided an example of a police-initiated project, in contrast to Cleveland and Derby, and was known to be making good progress in its inter-agency work. The Walsall Forum was also selected due to its geographical location and mix of minority ethnic communities. A further factor was that abused women were represented on the forum. No paid coordinator was in post. The local refuge was small and was not affiliated to Women's Aid. Thus, in various ways, this scenario contrasted with the situation in both Derby and Cleveland.

The policy and practice profile study areas

Choice of areas

■ Sheffield and South Yorkshire were selected as policy and practice profile areas due to the quite extensive inter-agency domestic violence work which had been conducted in Sheffield, and due to beginning the development of a strategy-making county-wide forum alongside the local domestic violence forums in South Yorkshire. The Sheffield Forum was more active than the other local forums, and both a general and an Asian women's refuge contributed to its work.

■ Dorset was selected due to extensive police involvement in the initiative, and to the rural and county-wide nature of the geographical area covered. There were only two refuges in the county, one of which was affiliated to WAFE. The inter-agency initiative was relatively new, but was developing quickly during the research period.

■ Bristol was selected as an example of a large city where the local authority had taken an initiating role but where multi-agency work was near the start of its development. Due to its size and other local characteristics, attempts to set up a city-wide domestic violence forum had fallen into abeyance as the research commenced. However, during the research period, small forums were established based in specific local communities which were independent of the original city group and of each other. The local refuge group, which runs both general refuges and a black women's refuge, was involved to some extent, but was not in a central position.

■ The London Borough of Greenwich was selected as an example of a metropolitan city area. During the mapping study, the local authority employed a coordinator for domestic violence issues. A very active local Women's Aid refuge and specialist Asian women's refuge participated in the forum, which developed swiftly during the research period due to the employment of the coordinator and despite extensive financial cutbacks in the borough.

■ North Wales was selected due to the fact that the forum there covered a large rural area containing more than one county. The forum had been initiated by a development officer in the probation service. It had benefited from extensive participation from the North Wales office of Welsh Women's Aid, the national federation representing Women's Aid refuges in Wales, and was unique in these respects.

Dissemination

■ Information from the research study was disseminated through a wide-ranging programme, which included speaking at conferences and seminars, attending domestic violence forum meetings, feeding back to refuge groups and women survivors of domestic violence, and producing papers and reports.

■ The research report is accompanied by a guide produced for practitioners (*Tackling domestic violence: a guide to developing multi-agency initiatives* –available from The Policy Press, University of Bristol, Rodney Lodge, Grange Road, Bristol BS8 4EA).

■ An edited book with both national and international content which reported on the research was also produced by two of the research team in conjunction with the national coordinator of WAFE.

■ A database and directory of inter-agency projects was produced. This database is held at WAFE and will be updated by them annually.

■ Formal reports were made to DDVAG, the Cleveland Multi-agency Domestic Violence Forum and the Walsall Domestic Violence Forum.

■ A Working Paper discussing the major issues emerging from the mapping study was produced in May 1995. This paper, written by the research team, is called *Against domestic violence: inter-agency initiatives*, and is also available from The Policy Press (Hague, Malos and Dear, 1995a).

■ The first national conference on domestic violence and inter-agency co-ordination, entitled 'Challenging violence against women: multi-agency initiatives to tackle domestic violence', was organised by the research team and WAFE, and held in June 1996.

■ It is planned to hold further conferences, workshops, seminars and training events on the research and on inter-agency work and domestic violence in the future.

Chapter 4

The initiatives in the study areas

Introduction

As discussed in previous chapters, the origin of multi-agency initiatives pre-dates official interest and encouragement although it has now picked up a further momentum from it. This shows in the varied beginnings of the 200 or so initiatives which were identified in our mapping survey, as well as those studied in greater depth during the main study period. These initiatives were often quite different in the various areas (Hague, Malos and Dear, 1995a; and see also Part II). They varied quite widely as to when they were set up and by whom, and in their structure and the scope and nature of the activities which they were planning and carrying out.

The variety of forms taken by the inter-agency forums in the study areas

Differences in origin would be expected to influence structures and ways of working, but this variety extended even to those forums which might be thought to be similar because they were initiated by the same statutory agency (eg, the police or probation service) in response to national stimulus.

One of the important, though not unexpected, findings emerging from the research was the way in which the origins, nature and shape taken by multi-agency initiatives, and the projects to which they gave rise, were influenced by local factors as well as by national policy and inter-

national practice. These local factors included existing relationships between agencies, existing networks, the strength or otherwise of women's community group activities (including refuge and advocacy services, Women's Aid groups and groups of black women and women from different minority ethnic communities), and the nature of the local community itself.

The differences and similarities between inter-agency structures and activities will be explored further in Part II, as will the question of how, given this variety and the existing pressure on agency resources, effective practice can be developed to support women who have experienced domestic violence and their children, to raise public awareness, and to challenge attitudes that give rise to domestic violence.

Getting started

There were wide variations in the way that the initiatives began, as well as in the shape they later took. These can be loosely classified according to the organisation or organisations which acted as the initial catalyst.

Women's Aid or community group network developments

Most initiatives were likely to have begun from a variety of agencies getting together. Sometimes this development resulted from a Women's Aid group stimulus in the very beginning, as in Cleveland, for example, where the forum arose from a meeting called by the Women's Aid group in Middlesbrough in 1991. According to a senior police officer who was interviewed in the course of the research, it was important that this meeting coincided with changes that were being made in police practice and policy locally, following the Home Office Circular in 1990, and that it took place in the context of the Women's Aid group's pre-existing work with police officers. Thus, in his view, the meeting led more easily to the development of multi-agency interest than might otherwise have been the case.

As in other initiatives, there was an initial phase of discussion of issues and building networks which was followed by the forum successfully obtaining funding, as noted, for a coordinator's post for the forum itself and for a local Zero Tolerance campaign, both of which assisted the forum to become much more action oriented. The funding came largely from Cleveland County Council, which has now been replaced, therefore raising some question marks over funding for the future.

Many multi-agency forums arise from already existing informal links. In Derby, for example, there were a series of multi-agency community workshops organised by the women's voluntary sector. Following concerns about levels of domestic violence, the local constabulary (together with refuge groups and other agencies) organised a workshop in 1991 attended by 37 agencies. At this point, DDVAG was set up.

Various initiatives were undertaken, but a number of members felt that the forum did not seem to be progressing beyond being principally a 'talking shop' (but see Holder, forthcoming, on the usefulness of discussion and of exchange of views between agencies to establish the extent, and limits, of the scope for common understandings and actions). The work of the forum was then stimulated by the obtaining of funding from the Derby Safer Cities project for a coordinator, which put it

on a much firmer basis. The brief of the forum expanded to encompass a wide model attempting to bring about institutional change, to establish broad links and to develop wide community awareness of domestic violence and its effects. One of the driving forces behind the establishment of this initiative, as already noted, was the part played by the local Women's Aid organisation, which provides support for all women and children experiencing domestic violence, including specialist support for black women and children and for women and children from minority ethnic communities. The forum has a particularly active management committee and an action-oriented strategy.

Local authority stimulus and backing

In some areas, local authority actions are of critical importance in stimulating, setting up and supporting multi-agency initiatives. This was the case in Greenwich, for example, where the London Borough of Greenwich Women's Equality Unit and Committee were of key importance in both respects. The forum was initiated jointly by the Equality Unit and the police. As previously noted, the coordinator for domestic violence issues, who is employed by the local authority Women's Equalities Unit, coordinates the forum, as one part of her duties, and active work on domestic violence of a variety of types has been initiated in the borough. The financial commitment by the local authority has been made despite a consistent year by year cutting back of the resources which it has had available in its central government grant. The social services department chairs the forum and plays a very active role, as do local refuges and the police. A parallel multi-agency group involving refuges and the local housing authority has developed to establish housing policy and training.

In Bristol, local authority action has also been important, with the Bristol City Council Housing Department initiating a city-wide forum in 1992/93. Initial meetings were held involving a number of voluntary and statutory agencies including the police (although there was no specialist domestic violence unit in the Police Authority area), but attendance tended to lack continuity and gradually decreased. In 1994, what was then the South Bristol Joint Operational Panel of Avon County Social Services Department organised the setting up of a local forum with representation from several agencies in the south of the city, especially health and social services, and with some police involvement. During the course of research another local forum has been set up in a district to the north of the city. This forum works with other voluntary and statutory partnership groups in the locality and contains solicitors, police officers, and social and community workers. A third local forum was being established as the research was completed. Although a central city-wide forum has not developed, the City Council has recently initiated a Zero Tolerance campaign. In addition, city-wide coordination may be possible in the future since the institution of a unitary authority in April 1996.

In Sheffield, the local domestic violence forum has benefited from very significant input from the City Council Community Safety Unit, which chaired the forum during the research period, and from the Council Equalities Unit. A wide variety of domestic violence initiatives have been instigated.

Police-initiated forums

In a few areas, multi-agency forums have developed at a county level on the initiative of senior police officers and others, as in South Yorkshire. Such county level forums may be combined with a number of more local forums. In South Yorkshire, for example, the county forum has attempted to work alongside forums in each of the four main towns (Sheffield, Rotherham, Doncaster and Barnsley). In some cases, a formal division of labour is envisaged with the county forum playing a strategic and policy role and the local forums being more practice and action oriented.

In such multi-level forums, borough or district councils or the probation service may play a significant initiating or co-ordinating role, along with the police. In South Yorkshire and Sheffield, for example, there has been a significant and active probation service element. Two domestic violence coordinators are currently employed in Sheffield, based in a probation office and funded by the Police Authority.

In Walsall and Dorset, the setting up of a police domestic violence unit with energetic and committed women officers was clearly of enormous importance in the establishment of the forum, although the precise shape of the initiative was strongly influenced by local factors in both cases. While the police took the responsibility for initiating the domestic violence forum in Walsall in 1992, a community support officer of Walsall Metropolitan Borough Council was a founder member of the forum, and other officers of the Borough Council from housing and social services departments also played a significant part in its development, as did the health authority. Unusually, the Benefits Agency played a significant role in the forum and developed its own good practice guidelines and extensive training designed to give a sensitive service to women who had experienced domestic violence and to protect their confidentiality and safety.

In Dorset where there was a county-wide forum in an area with significant urban populations in the south and east of the county, and an extensive rural hinterland in the west and north, there was less participation from district or county council departments other than social services. Local officers of some of the major voluntary agencies were actively involved, as were an officer of the local health commission and local solicitors. The two refuges in the county were sometimes able to send representatives, but regular attendance was difficult.

At the beginning in Dorset, a decision had been made to try to establish the forum in the more urban area around Bournemouth and Poole and to move on to develop a forum for the more rural districts later. This West Dorset Forum was set up after the fieldwork phase of this study had been completed.

Probation partnership initiatives

In some areas, as in North Wales, probation partnership initiatives were important in providing an impetus and an initial servicing role for setting up a forum, in a situation where the police were less active in taking up the policy and practice suggestions of Home Office Circular 60/90. There, a senior woman probation officer with crime prevention responsibilities was appointed to a development post in order to initiate partnership schemes. As part of this brief, she approached the Regional Office of the Welsh Women's Aid federation in September 1992.

At this point, a set of guidelines for the probation service on domestic violence (Association of Chief Officers of Probation, 1992, revised 1996) had been developed in consultation with WAFE following the National Inter-Agency Working Party (1992) but had not yet had wide circulation within probation or been taken up by North Wales Area Probation Service. However, the guidelines clearly offered important backing to the idea of a partnership between probation and other services and agencies relating to domestic violence. Following the consultation with Welsh Women's Aid, a forum was set up for the whole of the North Wales probation area involving two counties, with a base and basic servicing located in one of the area probation offices. However, it proved difficult in North Wales to move beyond networking to a more coordinated approach between agencies, despite extensive Women's Aid input. The forum has now decided that the two-county structure is too large for effective participation and is setting up new forums based on the areas of the unitary authorities.

Summary

■   As anticipated, the choice of research areas, although limited in number, allowed the study to consider a wide range of the issues arising in inter-agency initiatives on domestic violence. This presented challenges for the research in evaluating initiatives from very different places, set up for varying lengths of time and with varying levels of resources.

■   The initiatives were also often of considerable complexity in their membership base, varying in the spread of agencies represented and in the level of seniority of the representatives. They covered geographical areas of widely varying sizes.

■   In some cases, the forums had obtained funding for coordinators or other workers and then faced the challenge of acting as an effective employer, offering the right support and supervision. In others, where there was no funding even for basic servicing of meetings, there was sometimes a problem of continuity and development of the forum's work because of constraints on the time that agency workers could give. There was frustration, but also a great deal of experimentation and enthusiasm.

■ The study revealed a variety of strengths and weaknesses in the differing ways in which forums approached their work and tackled issues of structure, representation, and of equality between agencies and groups. Because domestic violence itself is such a complex phenomenon and touches so many areas, there were often philosophical and political as well as practical and operational issues to be overcome. The issues arising from these problems and challenges will be discussed in the following chapters.

Part II

Issues in multi-agency work

Chapter 5

Setting up and getting established

1. Are there distinct models of inter-agency domestic violence work?

1.1 As noted in the preceding chapter, inter-agency forums and their member agencies hold a wide variety of expectations about multi-agency work and what it can achieve. The wide-ranging evidence of the study indicates that this variety is reflected in a lack of uniform practice.

1.2 One of the aims of the research study was to investigate whether different models of inter-agency work on domestic violence issues exist. **Both the mapping study and the field work in the various study areas revealed that distinct models cannot be clearly distinguished from each other.**

1.3 **While many similarities exist between multi-agency initiatives in different localities, as already noted, these initiatives evolve in varying ways depending on local circumstances.** Thus, no two initiatives are the same. Local conditions identified by research respondents which may affect the development of inter-agency domestic violence work include historical, demographic, political and geographic factors, such as:

■ the presence or absence of refuges and specialist domestic violence projects;

■ the history of development of local Women's Aid groups and other refuges;

■ the commitment of local statutory agencies, including the local authority and its departments;

■ in particular, the strategy of the local police force in regard to setting up both domestic violence forums and also police domestic violence units;

■ the availability of resources;

■ the degree of activity of local women's groups and networks;

■ the presence or absence of specialist local authority units such as women's equality or community safety units;

■ the political complexion of the local authority;

■ the degree of agency commitment at senior management level;

■ the personalities, commitments and work priorities of local personnel. It was clearly evident from the research done that the importance of personalities should not be under-estimated.

2. Informal inter-agency work

2.1 **In several areas contacted during the mapping study, informal liaison, networking and coordination of service provision occurred without the establishment of a specific domestic violence initiative.** Women's Aid and other refuges have often engaged in this work for many years.

2.2 **Informal liaison of this type has value in itself.** Interview evidence from the research indicates that there may be no need for more formalised service co-ordination in the particular localities in question, where inter-agency liaison may have been occurring for a considerable period of time. In such situations, agencies and personnel may have established effective patterns of working together.

2.3 In other areas, multi-agency liaison may occur in relation to a specific one-off project. For example, a multi-agency group may be convened for a limited period of time to draw up some new practice guidance or to work on the setting up of a new refuge. Alternatively, inter-agency work may reoccur sporadically. For example, multi-agency child protection training on domestic violence may be held in a locality on an occasional basis.

3. Established inter-agency initiatives: first steps

3.1 Research respondents recommended that the first stage in forming an inter-agency initiative is to achieve as comprehensive representation from local agencies as is possible, bearing in mind local differences or difficulties, and providing the agencies concerned have some clear involvement in domestic violence work. The multi-agency group formed is often then known as a domestic violence forum, as previously noted.

3.2 Many domestic violence forums are set up as a result of an initial local conference or seminar called to discuss inter-agency coordination on a local level, and often involving speakers from more established initiatives, from the Women's Aid federations, and from local key agencies (eg, the police). Such conferences were held in York, Berkshire, Dorset, South Bristol, Staffordshire, Norwich and elsewhere, during the course of the research,

and in Surrey and Essex just before it commenced.

3.3 Some forums are set up as a result of a series of meetings or workshops involving relevant agencies which gradually move towards making a decision to set up an ongoing forum.

3.4 Alternatively, some forums are set up when a specialist worker comes into post, for example, in a local authority women's equality unit or community safety unit, who has a remit to establish multi-agency coordination. Such an officer may act as a catalyst and may be able to provide servicing for any multi-agency initiative which is established.

3.5 **Many local domestic violence forums have been set up by the police as part of initiatives to improve their response to domestic violence and to engage in multi-agency crime prevention initiatives.**

3.6 The research revealed that much dedicated and sensitive inter-agency work has been initiated by the police in various localities. However, interview evidence from both the mapping study and the detailed fieldwork also showed that some forums which were established and led by the police have experienced problems in involving voluntary sector agencies and in evolving a genuinely multi-agency response (see Section **17**).

3.7 In general, however, the research results suggest that the identity of the initiating agency, whether the police or any other organisation, does not seem to matter once the work has taken off and the group has 'gelled' together, providing that power differences between agencies are taken into account and that no one agency takes an overly dominating role. The research also offered tentative evidence that a positive factor in this respect is the active involvement of direct women's services, refuges and voluntary sector agencies.

3.8 Most initiatives studied were set up by groups of agencies working in concert, although the initiator was most commonly:

■ *Women's Aid and local refuges and women's advocacy services* (eg, Cleveland, North Manchester);

■ *the police* (eg, Walsall, West Midlands, Dorset);

■ *local authority women's equality, community safety, equal opportunity, citizens' or other specialist units* (eg, Hammersmith and Fulham, Waltham Forest, Sheffield, Islington, some of the Scottish Regions, Leeds);

■ *local authority departments* (eg, the original Bristol Domestic Violence Forum, which was initiated by Bristol City Council Housing Department).

3.9 However, a few forums were initiated by:

■ *the probation service* (eg, Staffordshire, Peterborough, North Wales);

■ *Victim Support* (eg, Bedfordshire, Gloucestershire);

■ *health providers* (eg, Salisbury, Charnwood);

■ *local solicitors firms* (eg, Chichester, Lawrence Weston in Bristol).

3.10 Most new forums work out ways of providing some sort of servicing or secretariat for themselves. For example, agencies attending may rotate taking the minutes and providing a venue, or one agency may take on this responsibility.

4. Who is involved

4.1 The major 'stake-holders' or 'players' in multi-agency domestic violence initiatives include both those which specialise in the issue (eg, Women's Aid) and those for which domestic violence work forms only a small percentage of their duties (eg, the

police and social services). It is important for involved agencies to be clear both about why they are there and how they might fit in to domestic violence work in general.

4.2 The extent of the commitment made often depends, according to study interviews, on whether or not an agency has a core responsibility for domestic violence and how that agency is governed by primary legislation concerning (or omitting) issues relating to the abuse of women in the home. For example, the police have a legal responsibility to police the criminal law on violent crime and assault, including domestic violence, and some aspects of the civil law, including parts of the domestic violence legislation. Social services, on the other hand, have no statutory responsibility for domestic violence, although it features prominently in their work, and the subject is omitted from key pieces of legislation, such as the 1989 Children Act. (The most active and prominent agencies involved in multi-agency domestic violence work in the study areas are listed in Table 1, p 25; see also Table 2, p 53 in Chapter 8). The main agencies involved in inter-agency initiatives are as follows (see also Sections **17-25**).

Women's Aid and other local women's refuge-based support and advocacy services

4.3 Women's Aid is widely accepted as being the lead specialist agency in domestic violence work, both in local areas and nationally. It is the major national organisation representing both abused women and children, and also activists and practitioners. The four Women's Aid federations take a national role in policy making and coordinate networks of affiliated refuge and advocacy services in England, Scotland, Wales and Northern Ireland. Some refuges are not affiliated to the Women's Aid federations and remain independent, separately managed by housing associations, by church-related bodies or by specialist organisations, for example, Asian women's groups. Both generalist refuges and also specialist refuges, for example, for black women and children, and for women and children from minority ethnic communities, exist.

Other women's and community organisations

4.4 These include community groups, women's advice and support groups, black women's groups, disabled women's groups, rape crisis centres, projects for homeless women, lesbians, women in crisis, etc. Local campaigning organisations and women's networks, which have been formed particularly to work on issues of violence against women, may also be included. The Brighton and Hove Domestic Violence Forum was set up, for example, by a local campaign group against domestic violence.

The local authority

4.5 Many local authorities take an active role in inter-agency work on domestic violence. As noted in **1.3** and **3.8**, this involvement is most often mediated through small specialist units, such as *equality*, w*omen's equality* or c*ommunity safety units*.

Of the major departments, *housing* and *social services departments* are the most usually involved. However, evidence from the mapping study indicates that social services departments in some areas have been slow to participate, due in part to their lack of clear statutory responsibility in respect of domestic violence. Housing departments are also absent in some areas despite their responsibilities in regard to homelessness and domestic violence.

Local authority *education departments* are much less often involved in inter-agency domestic violence initiatives, although some are now developing educational materials and programmes as discussed in Section **16**. Local councillors are involved in some forums and, in a few cases, take the chair.

The police

4.6 The police service has a major part to play in responding to domestic violence as the foremost 24-hour emergency service. As noted, the police have taken a particularly active role in promoting and developing domestic violence forums throughout the country, although with regional variations (see Sections **3.5** and Sections **3.6**), and are the most widely represented of all agencies on local multi-agency initiatives. Most commonly, although by no means always, participation in domestic violence forums is mediated through dedicated domestic violence units or officers.

Probation

4.7 The probation service is involved in many domestic violence forums, most often where abusers programmes for men on probation are in operation, or are in the process of being set up, or where partnership projects involving responses to domestic violence are being established.

The Crown Prosecution Service

4.8 The Crown Prosecution Service (CPS) participates in some domestic violence forums. However, a very large number of groups contacted for this study noted its absence. Representatives of the CPS rarely attended forum meetings in these areas.

Victim Support

4.9 Both locally and nationally, Victim Support is involved in inter-agency initiatives on domestic violence as a result of its role in supporting victims of crime. This interest is in line with the new emphasis within the police and the rest of the criminal justice system on viewing domestic violence as a crime.

Table 1: Participation in inter-agency forums – agencies most prominent and active in the study areas

	Cleveland	Derby	Walsall	Sheffield	Greenwich	Dorset	North Wales	Bristol† Forum 1	Bristol† Forum 2
Police	✓	✓	✓	✓	✓	✓	✓	✓	✓
Police domestic violence unit	✓	✓	✓	✓	✓	✓			
Probation	✓	✓		✓			✓		
Family Court Welfare			✓						
Court Personnel									
Local authority special unit*	✓	✓		✓	✓			✓	✓
Local authority social services departments	✓	✓	✓	✓	✓	✓	✓	✓	
Local authority housing departments and housing bodies	✓	✓	✓	✓	✓			✓	
Local authority education department				✓					
Health services	✓		✓	✓		✓			✓
Benefits Agency			✓	✓		✓			
Women's Aid refuges	✓	✓	✓	✓	✓	✓	✓	✓	✓
Specialist refuges (eg, for black women and children)		✓	✓	✓	✓			✓	✓
Other refuges		✓	✓	✓					
Victim Support			✓	✓		✓	✓	✓	✓
Children's charities	✓		✓	✓		✓			
Relate	✓	✓				✓		✓	✓
Community organisations (including women's, disability and black community groups)	✓	✓	✓	✓	✓	✓	✓	✓	✓
Youth projects		✓		✓		✓			
Other voluntary sector projects	✓	✓	✓	✓	✓	✓		✓	
Solicitors		✓	✓	✓		✓	✓		✓

* Local authority special units may include community safety, women's equality or other similar units. † Forum 1 is in South Bristol; Forum 2 is in Lawrence Weston in North Bristol.

Other voluntary sector organisations

4.10 A variety of voluntary sector groups, for example, children's organisations, may participate in multi-agency initiatives. Housing associations and other housing organisations are often active in domestic violence forums.

Health service professionals

4.11 Health service professionals participate in some domestic violence forums although, during the mapping study, their absence was noted far more frequently than their presence.

Solicitors

4.12 Some solicitors and other professionals in private practice, wishing to go beyond their professional legal role and to take on domestic violence in a more comprehensive manner, may participate in domestic violence forums. In general, during the mapping survey, legal personnel, court officers, judges and magistrates were noted in their absence.

5. Getting agreement and making decisions

5.1 Member agencies in the forums investigated were notable in terms of the large numbers of differences between them. Since some member agencies may have little basic information about domestic violence, a useful starting point can be to engage jointly in a multi-agency training session on domestic violence awareness. Such training may be repeated on a recurring basis for new agencies in order for agencies to learn from each other and to expand their knowledge about the issues and dilemmas facing abused women and children.

5.2 One of the main initial tasks facing a new domestic violence forum is to develop links and contacts between individuals and agencies. Many forums contacted during the research met for a long period, often more than one year, and sometimes several years, predominantly to exchange information and to build networks. (For a further discussion of this issue, see Section **10**.)

5.3 After a phase of networking, however, many forums move on to attempt to develop *guiding principles* to which all can agree, as a part of evolving some form of coordinated action. Examples of *guiding principles* documents are included in Appendix B, pp 92-96. They frequently contain a definition of domestic violence as agreed by members and include commitments to view domestic violence as a crime, to take action to combat and prevent it, to provide co-ordinating services to assist abused women and children in a non-judgemental manner, and to integrate equalities issues into their work. The most important of these principles is generally that inter-agency cooperation aims to decrease or prevent domestic violence and to increase the safety of abused women and children. (How successful domestic violence forums are at fulfilling these goals is discussed in Section **28**. See also the section on *aims and objectives*, in particular, Section **6.2**.) Interviewees pointed out that it can be useful if participating agencies 'sign up' in writing to indicate their acceptance of the principles which have been agreed.

5.4 Working on *guiding principles* may be the first task in which forum members engage together. The development of a set of principles of this type can involve dealing with philosophical and operational differences between agencies and differing attitudes to domestic violence. Resolving such differences without resorting to a 'lowest common denominator' situation, and while attempting to build trust and honesty, was singled out by various interviewees in all the study areas as a major issue in conducting inter-agency work.

5.5 Women's Aid and the refuge movement have been at the forefront of work to combat domestic violence for more than 20 years and have evolved understandings of violence against women which are now being adopted by other agencies (Barron, Harwin and Singh, 1992; National Inter-Agency Working Party, 1992; Home Affairs Committee, 1993). As a result, the analysis presented by Women's Aid is frequently discussed in multi-agency forums when *guiding principles* are being developed, even when there is no refuge in the area. This analysis includes an understanding of gender inequality and of issues of power and control between men and women in relation to domestic violence. It also includes a philosophy of working towards the empowerment of women and children in practical ways, and a commitment to self-help and self-determination for women and children and to equal opportunities. Further, Women's Aid principles emphasise the central importance of the abused woman's perspective in the provision of support and services; the value of the mutual support of other women who have similar experiences; and a commitment to caring for the emotional, developmental and educational needs of children affected by domestic violence.

5.6 In most of the study areas, statutory and voluntary sector agencies worked closely with Women's Aid and accepted their expertise as specialists in the field. However, contention around Women's Aid's views existed in some localities. In a large number of areas contacted during the mapping study, local refuges felt marginalised in the inter-agency initiative, as though, in the words of an interviewee: "their voices are not heard". Conversely, in two of the study areas, a few interviewees from other agencies felt badgered by Women's Aid on occasion. In other forums contacted during the mapping study, Women's Aid was not adequately represented at meetings and so was unable to enter the debate. In several areas, Women's Aid representatives believed that they had to be constantly vigilant in order to avoid the overlooking of their analysis or its dilution beyond recognition. These complex issues are more fully discussed in Section **25**.

5.7 **Resolving differences of opinion and philosophy about understandings of, and responses to, domestic violence specifically is an essential task for any meaningful multi-agency initiative.** Differences may develop as a result of conflicting views about domestic violence against men, for example, or about practice responses to abused women and children (for instance, concerning conciliation with partners or about prevalence of, and ways of responding to, sexual abuse). **Research interviewees pointed out that these differences are often played out through differences in power between member agencies, with small organisations frequently feeling, or being, marginalised or pushed to one side.**

> "The multi-agency forum needs to make sure all agencies know about it and get the literature and send representatives. The forum needs to go on doing this – persuading agencies to get involved. 'Background organising' needs to be done all the time to involve small organisations.... Everywhere, small voluntary groups may be silenced and overlooked by large meetings when the big statutory agencies dominate." (Agency interviewee, Cleveland)

5.8 **On the other hand, some representatives of large statutory agencies interviewed for the study felt that the view of them which was adopted by small voluntary agencies and campaigning groups was too narrow and stereotyped to allow for growth and change.**

5.9 Various inter-agency forums make use of consultants from domestic violence training agencies, from the Women's Aid federations and from academic institutions in attempting to resolve these issues and specifically to develop basic principles, aims, written documents and structures.

5.10 Even where basic agreement has been achieved on guiding principles and on the goals of a multi-agency domestic violence initiative, the research provided evidence that the development of inter-agency co-operation demands careful communication skills and inter-personal interaction.

> "It can be hard – you can get 'grid-lock'. You need to be able to talk about things together and agencies need to really listen to each other." (Agency interviewee, Greenwich)

The potentially explosive and divisive nature of such a painful topic as domestic violence can combine with these inter-personal issues and with complex features of group dynamics to produce very difficult situations within domestic violence forums. In several forums contacted during the research, employed workers had resigned at short notice after disputes, or inter-personal disagreement had led to members leaving the group or refusing to attend.

5.11 In one of the study areas, such inter-personal problems combined with strong religious beliefs had led to considerable difficulties involving a particular staff member. In another, what was described by some as an over-strident expression of particular views by a few members had led to disillusion among others who had felt "put down and belittled" as a result. **Research interviews provided some evidence that less combative discussions and respectful, careful presentation of opinions could have a more successful outcome than forceful challenge, without necessarily sacrificing honesty.**

5.12 The use of facilitators, of team building training, of good communication skills, and of careful open

discussion over time can assist in avoiding such difficulties and in evolving an atmosphere of trust. In addition, interviewees described how members from different agencies sometimes make a decision "to agree to differ". In these situations, it was useful if there was clarity between all participants about which areas were covered by such an agreement and which were not.

5.13 Some difficulties and disagreements which revealed themselves during the research involved equalities issues. Examples include an ignoring of cultural diversity and class issues by some forum members and in work taken on; an overlooking of equality practice on which decisions had previously been made (eg, that all venues should have disabled access); and the frequently mentioned experience of black, disabled or lesbian members of local forums feeling overlooked or not taken seriously by other members. The research team engaged in various discussions and meetings about these issues which confirmed that resolving equality issues is often painful for all concerned and can be particularly so in a multi-agency setting where agencies may be tempted to defend their own 'turf' (their ethos, views and working practices), and where equal opportunities practice will have developed to different degrees in different organisations. These issues are fully discussed in Section **26**.

5.14 In this context, in some of the study areas, interviewees felt that the actual structure of the forum meetings could be uninviting to small voluntary sector groups and that this could have implications in terms of equal opportunities. Some small black agencies, for example, might not wish to attend a large mainly white group. In at least two of the study areas, attempts to involve such agencies had met with very limited success, the domestic violence forum being apparently regarded by some local community groups as a "white, middle class organisation".

5.15 Similar difficulties were sometimes described by interviewees in relation to the involvement in large forum meetings of women who had experienced domestic violence. While many forums include members who are domestic violence survivors, these participants most commonly are attending in other capacities as professionals. The multi-agency forum in Hounslow is an example of a woman-only forum and has, from the outset, involved women who have experienced violence. This issue is being given attention in several of the study areas (as discussed in Section **27**).

5.16 Many domestic violence forums attempt to make decisions by consensus. Some use specific techniques to enable all to participate equally. Examples are:

■ going round the meeting so that each agency can take a turn and participate in discussions;

■ making sure that particular agencies do not dominate discussions and decision making, except in so far as they possess greater expertise and knowledge (eg, specialist domestic violence projects and refuges may be acknowledged as the experts on the issue by other agencies);

■ acknowledging shared responsibility for decision making openly, in all work done, all documents produced, etc.

5.17 Some forums did not move ahead until complete full agreement and consensus had been reached on all issues (eg, the Stirling Multi-agency Domestic Violence Project; see also Moelwyn-Hughes, forthcoming), although this could create difficulties over the amount of time taken to reach decisions and often conflicted with methods of working in some member agencies.

5.18 Some forums have discussed adopting more imaginative methods to avoid the emphasis on long meetings, which can be alienating to some participants, and to enable multi-agency gatherings to be more dynamic, to be sensitive to class, cultural and disability issues, and to include variations in use of language. However, the study revealed little practical information on actual attempts to carry out such plans.

5.19 Rather, forum members often complained that the number of meetings being called tended to increase and could become unmanageable. Participants frequently had limited personal and work resources to commit to the project and could not afford the time and energy needed to achieve full consensus or to go over issues sufficiently thoroughly to achieve a collective ethos and identity. However, considerable strides had been made in these directions in several of the study areas. DDVAG, for example, and others have engaged in 'away day' team building training and exercises with an outside facilitator. **It was clear from the study evidence that techniques to improve decision making and communication need to be constantly monitored for effectiveness, and that the effectiveness of decision making overall needs to be regularly monitored and evaluated.**

Summary

■ No distinct models of inter-agency work exist and no two initiatives are the same. While many similarities exist, multi-agency initiatives in different areas evolve in varying ways depending on local circumstances, personnel and conditions.

■ Informal liaison and networking has value in itself. Where good informal coordination exists, there may be no need for a more formalised approach.

■ The first stage in establishing a multi-agency initiative is getting the commitment of as comprehensive a range of statutory and voluntary sector organisations as possible, providing these agencies have some clear involvement in domestic violence work. The identity of the initiating agency does not appear to matter if the group 'gels', if power differences are taken into account, and if no one agency 'leads' or dominates.

■ The major 'stake-holders' in multi-agency domestic violence initiatives include both those who specialise in domestic violence work and those for whom it is not a core part of their work, with their involvement varying accordingly. It is important for involved agencies to be clear both about why they are there and how they might fit into domestic violence work in general.

■ Involved agencies include Women's Aid and other refuges, women's and community organisations, the police, local authority specialist units (eg, community safety or equality units), local authority housing and social services departments (to a rather variable extent) and occasionally councillors, the probation service, Victim Support, solicitors and voluntary sector agencies. During the mapping study, local education departments, the CPS, and legal and court personnel were seldom involved. Health care providers and other health service professionals were absent in a surprisingly large number of cases.

■ Member agencies of domestic violence forums are notable in the differences between them. Initial domestic violence awareness training can assist agencies in increasing their knowledge about domestic violence and starting to build a joint approach. Many forums then meet for more than a year, or for several years, as networking groups.

■ Many develop a set of *guiding principles*, which can involve dealing with philosophical and operational differences between agencies. Resolving such differences without resorting to a 'lowest common denominator' situation was identified as a major issue in conducting inter-agency work. Differences of opinion and philosophy about understandings of, and responses to, domestic violence could be a specific issue of difficulty. These differences are often played out through differences in power between member agencies.

■ Even where basic agreement has been achieved on goals and principles, the research provided evidence that the development of inter-agency cooperation demands careful and sensitive communication skills and inter-personal interaction. In some cases, agencies make a decision "to agree to differ" on specified issues.

■ The use of facilitators, of team building training, of good communication skills, and of careful, open and honest discussion over time can assist in avoiding difficulties and in working towards a common vision. Many domestic violence forums attempt to make decisions by consensus. Some use specific techniques to enable all to participate equally, which need to be constantly monitored for effectiveness. In general, the effectiveness of decison making needs to be regularly monitored and evaluated.

Chapter 6

Structure and organisational issues

6. Structure and management of domestic violence forums and initiatives

6.1   As domestic violence forums evolve, many develop *aims and objectives*. These tend to cover general issues about combating domestic violence and viewing it as a crime, about increasing the safety of abused women and children, about integrating equalities issues into the work of the forum, and about engaging preventative and educational work in service coordination. Such general aims are usually supplemented by specific and more easily achievable objectives. Examples of *aims and objectives* documents are included in Appendix B, pp 92-96.

6.2   The study accumulated evidence to suggest strongly that the underlying aim of all domestic violence forums should be to improve women and children's safety and to combat domestic violence. However, some groups in the study appeared to have lost sight of this basic aim in a plethora of meetings. Monitoring mechanisms to ensure that it remains centre-stage clearly need to be put in place in such circumstances.

6.3   Forums may go on to develop more comprehensive *terms of reference*. These may include *mission statements* and other documents. *Equal opportunities policies* form an important part of *terms of reference*. Examples of such policies are included in Appendix B, pp 92-96.

6.4   Many domestic violence forums do not have constitutions, although some investigated during the research were in the process of becoming constituted (eg, Walsall). As noted in Section **9**, some were set up as voluntary sector organisations, as limited companies, or had been granted charitable status, while others remained as networks or as organisations operating under the auspices of one agency.

6.5   As domestic violence forums become more established, many create a formal structure. Most commonly, this consists of a smaller steering group or steering committee (sometimes known as a management committee) to manage the day-to-day running of the initiative on behalf of the whole forum. The full domestic violence forum is then likely to meet less frequently, for example, every six weeks or every three months. Steering committees usually include representatives of the most involved of the local agencies, including refuges, and have a chairperson and other elected officers. The adoption of specific job descriptions for steering committee members and officers has occurred in some forums (eg, Derby), and has introduced clarity and consistency.

6.6   In general, steering committees need to have an active consistent representative membership, to be elected if possible, to be accountable to the full membership and to develop clear procedures and lines of accountability.

6.7 Some forums, however, continue to meet as a full group for several years and find no need for the establishment of a separate steering group (eg, Greenwich during the research period).

6.8 Many forums establish sub-groups to progress different types of work. Sometimes these are ongoing groups (eg, a legal sub-group). Sometimes they are concerned with a particular piece of work (eg, organising a conference or drawing up specific practice guidelines). During the research period, the Walsall Domestic Violence Forum operated Staffing, Training, Funding and Media/Publicity Sub-committees. It had also established an Elderly Person's Task Group. The Cleveland Multi-agency Forum operated Training, Funding and Children's Needs Sub-groups. The Greenwich Domestic Violence Forum operated an Asian Women's Sub-group, and also a Working with Women Sub-group, a Working with Men Sub-group and a Children's and Young People's Sub-group. In Dorset there was a Public Awareness Sub-group and a Resources Directory Sub-group. North Wales had a Conference Sub-group, a Training Sub-group and a Directory Sub-group. In the Sheffield Forum, in addition to sub-groups on employment, finance and training, an Anti-oppressive Practice Sub-group had been established.

6.9 Findings from the mapping study indicate that sub-groups can work particularly well if participation in them is time-limited with a specific task to accomplish. The original Nottingham-shire Domestic Violence Forum, for example, operated each sub-group for a one-year period only. Members could then make a realistic commitment to participate and could build it into their work plans for a set period.

6.10 Some forums operated sub-groups dealing with a specialist area of work which were very successful. One example is the North Wales Domestic Violence Forum

Training Sub-group which, in common with other training sub-groups, is ongoing. Another is the Children's Needs Sub-group in Cleveland, which operated while the county of Cleveland was still in existence (see pp 43-44). Some sub-groups have a 'watching brief' to look at policy and practice on specialised topics.

6.11 One of the main points made to the researchers about sub-groups was that consistency of attendance and commitment from participants and a clear remit are necessary in order to facilitate effective action. Sub-groups also need to have access through the operation of clear procedures to any relevant resources that the forum may have.

6.12 Interviewees in one of the research areas made the point that the status of sub-groups in relation to the whole forum can become blurred and that it is important to keep lines of accountability clear, and understood by all participants. In general, the point was made to the researchers that, because of the potential in a complex multi-agency operation for confusion and misunderstandings, clarity is required between all members in regard to all issues of structure, responsibility and accountability.

6.13 In order to progress the work, several of the initiatives in the study areas developed *action plans*. These could be quite complex, as in Walsall and Greenwich. In some areas, the *action plan* was reviewed at each forum meeting to monitor progress in different areas of work and to maintain clarity (as in Greenwich) which had led to a focused development of the work done. Once a forum has a clear remit and plan, research interviewees point out that the group needs to ensure that this focus is not lost or diluted by the participation of agencies without a direct contribution to make.

6.14 There is a trend within multi-agency initiatives to conduct a *service audit*. Each agency in a forum commits itself to conduct an audit of its policies and practice on domestic violence, which may lead on to the development of an individual *action plan* within each agency. Simultaneously, collective activities and action involving several agencies working in concert can be developed.

6.15 A lack of "thinking strategically" and of evolving longer term *strategic plans* had apparently impeded progress in some areas. Some of the better established forums had evolved three- or five-year *strategic plans* which had enabled effective project development.

6.16 The effectiveness of multi-agency forums in meeting their *aims and objectives* appeared during the research study to be an issue of contention. Interviewees in various research areas suggested that forums need to constantly monitor and assess their effectiveness in two major respects:

a) their effectiveness in meeting and in highlighting the needs of women and children experiencing domestic violence;

b) the effectiveness of the structures and processes which they operate specifically in enabling (a).

7. Gaining influence

7.1 In order to develop an influential presence locally, forums need to evolve a clear identify. The research showed that consistency of attendance and of commitment to the forum by member agencies and their officers were of key importance in evolving this identity. Getting each agency to take the initiative seriously, to make a commitment to it and to send delegated representatives (rather than to rely on ad hoc personal interest) were major tasks in all the research areas.

> "Different agencies – different priorities: there is a lot of potential for different positions being taken, for some agencies feeling defensive; then it's a problem about agencies giving it credence, importance. The level of credibility with different agencies is not high sometimes. There's a problem of people sometimes attending despite, rather than because of, their agency, the agency not being interested in it. Or, then again, some agencies only attend to gain kudos and say they are doing something when they're not, to cover up inaction.... There's a great potential for muddling through, poor decision making...." (Agency interviewee, policy and practice study area)

7.2 The research showed that forums can usefully develop a recognisable profile locally. This can include engaging in publicity exercises and attempting to build a good local reputation and 'portfolio' of activities.

7.3 One of the strengths of domestic violence inter-agency initiatives is often their grass-roots dynamism. However, gaining influence locally frequently involves the commitment of senior or policy-making officers within the local authority, the police force, the probation service and other agencies.

> "We want people at the sharp end not those in their ivory towers. It's not good them sending a manager who has not dealt with the public for ten years. That's no solution – we can achieve more with the up-front workers being there ... but it needs management to say it is imperative we have formal representation on the forum and not leave it to the individuals to decide if it is one of their priorities. It must be seen as part of the post." (Agency interviewee, Walsall)

7.4 Different forums have approached the difficulty of both ensuring grass-roots or front-line participation and also gaining influence with and commitment from management and local policy makers in different ways. Some have maintained their grass-roots community base while setting up an ongoing structure of regular policy meetings or conferences with senior officers in the relevant agencies.

7.5   Many forums contain a mixture of practitioners and policy makers in order to overcome the problem. However, holding this situation in balance can be problematic. While a strong commitment to maintaining community and practitioner involvement had been made in the majority of the study areas, in some it was felt that the decision making and policy making power of members representing statutory bodies was not sufficiently great for them to be able to make commitments on behalf of their agencies or to instigate effective improvement in policy and practice.

7.6   In various areas, a corporate response to domestic violence has been formulated across a local authority, sometimes through the establishment of a working group of officers from the various departments, into which local domestic violence forums can feed information and ideas.

7.7   In some areas, senior level multi-agency strategy-making groups have been established, specifically to evolve local strategy on domestic violence, but sometimes cut off from practitioner, community or refuge networks.

7.8   Broader experiments with county-wide strategy-making multi-agency forums involving senior officers, informed by smaller local practitioner forums, have been tried in some counties and have met with limited success so far. The development of a coordinated local or regional domestic violence strategy is clearly an outcome to be welcomed.

7.9   However, the following possible difficulties with such a two-tier system were identified during the study:

■   possible duplication of organisational effort and work done;

■   the same officers may end up attending both local and regional forums;

■   officers may be insufficiently senior to be in a position to influence the evolution of wider strategy;

■   senior officers may attend but be unable to prioritise or take a real interest in the issue, or to make realistic commitments to it, due to other pressures;

■   senior officers may be cut off from, and may not 'take on board' information from, practitioners and grass-roots agencies;

■   regional or county forums may look good but do little (sometimes because of distances involved and top-heavy structures);

■   forums of this type may be less advanced than local urban forums on such issues as equalities;

■   introducing another tier of meetings can lead to an additional level of bureaucracy which new initiatives have to pass through.

7.10   However, there are advantages to setting up a county-wide strategy level forum, especially since some agencies have a county-wide remit. In South Yorkshire, the plan has been to develop a county forum of senior officers who, together with representatives of the local forums, can draw up corporate and county-wide domestic violence strategies. Similar plans are in progress in other areas (eg, Derbyshire). The development of strategy-making forums of this type would ensure that domestic violence work was taken seriously throughout a region or county and was a feature of coordinated planning between agencies across the area in question.

7.11 In North Wales, the forum extends over a two-county area, similar to the local probation service, but is being reorganised on a district basis. Some forums fit in with the areas covered by particular agencies (eg, the police), rather than by a local authority. Some are set up in smaller local areas (eg, the small forums in areas of Bristol). The areas served by domestic violence initiatives may change further in the future with the setting up of unitary authorities. The Cleveland Multi-agency Forum, for example, which previously covered Cleveland County, now remains as an over-arching forum with four local forums developing in the four new unitary authorities.

8. Resourcing

8.1 During the study, lack of resources was the single largest factor inhibiting the development of local inter-agency work on domestic violence. Interviewees in all study areas were more or less unanimous on this score. **Many pointed to the lack of provision for resources in the 1995 Home Office Inter-agency Circular. The majority of the statutory agencies participating in the inter-agency initiatives studied were themselves facing considerable funding cut-backs and contraction of services, and sometimes could not justify involvement in domestic violence forums unless such involvement could be designated as 'core' work.** Health services, police forces and local authorities were all facing such difficulties in most of the study areas. It could then be difficult to prioritise domestic violence work.

8.2 Some statutory agencies attempted to donate resources to their local forum, providing venues, for example, or rotating the forum secretariat between them, but the research team was informed of many instances where this work was apparently becoming less possible due to increasing pressure of other work. **Voluntary sector members and refuges were rarely in a position to donate resources.**

8.3 However, the vast majority of inter-agency initiatives have no resources at all, apart from what participating agencies can donate or share. During the study period, for example, the Bristol forums were in this situation and work had been substantially slowed down as a result, although some dynamic developments had occurred in the local communities concerned. There was also the problem in many areas of raising expectations by establishing and publicising the forum and then being unable to meet these expectations due to lack of resources.

> "We must take a step at a time and not run before we can walk. It is important not to raise expectations beyond resources and not build up false hopes for women, as that could be very damaging." (Agency interviewee, Walsall)

8.4 Forums which were in receipt of some funding had obtained it from a variety of sources, including various local authority committees, the Police Authority, partnership initiatives, the Home Office Safer Cities Scheme, and other similar sources. No common pattern of funding emerged in the study. This funding situation has led to a piecemeal approach in which local projects may struggle to obtain a 'basket' of local finance, obtaining small amounts of funding from a variety of sources. Success in obtaining any resources at all in the areas investigated in both the mapping survey and the main study was often only achieved after large amounts of voluntary and time-consuming fund-raising by forum members. In addition, funding for coordinators and other workers was invariably short term, precipitating recurring funding crises. Thus, financial uncertainty and insecurity prevailed in almost all funded initiatives, according to the study evidence. This resource situation militates against constructive forward-planning and project development, and, on a general level, against inter-agency domestic violence initiatives fulfilling their potential.

8.5 Even where domestic violence forums have access to paid co-ordinators, raising funds to resource activities undertaken frequently continues to be a problem. In various research areas, this situation had resulted in a great deal of work for the fund-raisers in the project, often without positive results. This was the case in Greenwich, Derby, and in other localities during the research period, and as a result, planned work has had to be abandoned or cut back due to lack of resources (although the Derby project has been successful in securing some resources for activities in addition to short-term funding for its employees).

8.6 Better coordination of existing services on a small scale and improvement of practice within member agencies can occur without outside resources. However, further coordination work and engagement in specific activities and programmes of work have inevitable resource implications.

8.7 Within this situation of lack of resources, most research respondents believed that local funding for refuges and emergency services for abused women and children should take priority over inter-agency work. **Current best practice is clearly that multi-agency projects should not compete with Women's Aid and the refuge movement for grant-aid, but rather should engage actively in attempting to ensure that these services are adequately resourced. Many initiatives make it a priority to facilitate the development and funding of refuges and emergency advocacy and support services.** Ideally, interviewees pointed out that the provision of direct services, and the development of educative and preventative work and inter-agency coordination, should

go hand-in-hand as different sides of the same coin. It makes no sense if they are competitors. In addition, the point was made that the conducting of inter-agency awareness-raising work in a locality can act as a vital catalyst to increased funding for the provision of refuges and direct services. Nevertheless, the current lack of resources, and the need to compete for them, has introduced a difficult situation. During the course of the research, the inter-agency projects in two of the main study areas found themselves to be in direct competition with local refuge providers for small amounts of grant-aid. Further difficulties of this sort may be anticipated in the future.

9. Employment of workers

9.1 The study accumulated strong evidence from many areas of the country that the employment of a coordinator or a development worker was of key importance in progressing inter-agency domestic violence work. Research interviews were unanimous throughout the study that, while agencies could work together to coordinate their services and to engage in some joint work without the assistance of a paid worker, the employment of a coordinator could have a transforming effect upon the project. The great majority of interviewees felt that only the most minimal inter-agency co-ordination could take place otherwise. **Even so, it should be noted that most forums across the country do not have employees.**

9.2 Several of the domestic violence forums in the research areas selected for this study either had access to paid co-ordinators, as described in Chapter 3, or the staff of participating agencies could service the forum to some extent as a recognised part of their work. Coordinators could be specially employed workers as in Sheffield, Derby and Cleveland. In North Wales, local coordination was provided by the probation service and Welsh Women's Aid. In Greenwich, the local authority-employed coordinator for domestic violence issues worked on behalf of the domestic violence forum as one part of her overall duties. The two small local forums in Bristol did not have paid coordinators, although this function was fulfilled in an unpaid capacity by other professionals. The Walsall Forum also had no coordinator and, while local agencies including Health Promotion, Victim Support and the police were very active, the lack of a coordinator was much regretted.

9.3 In areas where coordinators were in post, interviewees described how this had enabled the inter-agency initiative to become fully established and to initiate a variety of types of project which would have been impossible previously. **According to interviewees, a coordinator was able to give a domestic violence forum presence, focus and direction, and to do behind-the-scenes networking and contacting to 'oil' the inter-agency process.** Interviewees in Derby, Cleveland, Sheffield and elsewhere pointed out that it can be helpful if the person employed has some experience of Women's Aid and the refuge movement, a background in women's organisations and services, and an understanding of the gendered power dynamics of domestic violence.

9.4 However, interviewees also noted that the coordinator's role is to support and facilitate the project, rather than to lead it. The ideas fuelling the forum need ideally to come from service providers and practitioners rather than from the coordinator, so that the steering committee, where there is one, leads the project, informed by the forum membership.

9.5 The first few domestic violence forums and inter-agency projects in this country were coordinated (on either a paid or an unpaid basis) by workers of considerable vision and personal charisma.

Now, however, interviewees in Hammersmith, Fulham and elsewhere, pointed out that the initial pioneering stage of this work in Britain is over. Nevertheless, coordinators need to fulfil a considerable range of personal and employment specifications. **Research respondents were asked about the qualities necessary, and listed a variety of tasks which need to be fulfilled by a coordinator as an organiser, as a spokesperson and publicist for the project, as a protagonist on behalf of abused women and children, and as an administrator and planner, with vision for the project and for the future.**

> "A coordinator must be confident and able to find her way around and motivated, being resourceful is very important. Also 'oiling' the works! Brokering the forum to resolve philosophical and political difficulties – 'oiling' is needed…. Political conflicts can happen. Conflict can be creative though in a forum." (Interviewee, Derby)

9.6 In sum, these qualities were described to the researchers as including:

■ good coordinating and administrative skills;

■ good networking skills to bring agencies together and to smooth out difficulties;

■ the ability to work closely with refuges;

■ the ability to work with, and be taken seriously by, senior managers and policy makers, and by the statutory sector as a whole;

■ the ability to work with, and be taken seriously by, grass-roots projects and community groups;

■ the ability to promote and publicise the project throughout the locality;

■ the ability to deal sensitively with issues of equal opportunity;

■ a background in women's services and domestic violence work, as noted.

9.7 Interview evidence from various parts of the country, accumulated as part of the study, indicates that the employment of a coordinator alone, without any administrative support, is often insufficient to enable the initiative to develop effectively. The employment of an administrator or administrative assistant, or the provision of administrative or secretarial help for the coordinator, was viewed as being extremely helpful by a variety of interviewees. **When asked what the minimum level of support would be, many suggested a full-time coordinator and a part-time or full-time administrative assistant or project support officer.** DDVAG has adopted this employment strategy, and obtained resources to fund it, to the clear benefit of the initiative.

9.8 Employment structures vary for domestic violence forums. **For some, the coordinator is a local authority employee (as in Greenwich) or the post is 'hosted' by the authority (as in Cleveland).** This could be a very beneficial arrangement according to interviewees, providing that the hosting agency did not then start to 'own' the work done. Most frequently, workers of this type are based in an equalities unit or a community safety unit. **Other inter-agency initiatives are situated firmly in the voluntary sector with a voluntary steering or management committee**, as noted in Section **6**. This arrangement was favoured by many interviewees as it enabled the initiative to be independent.

As discussed earlier, many are neither constituted nor incorporated as a distinct body, which can cause problems for employment unless a member agency is willing to provide employee management.

9.9 Where workers are employed through a local authority or other agency, that agency will be responsible for management and supervision. It appears from the research that such employee management is usually provided sympathetically, although problems can arise in that a multi-agency worker is being managed by just one of the agencies involved. Where the project is based in the voluntary sector, a variety of employee management styles are possible, ranging from those which are participatory and 'open' to those which are tightly hierarchical. **In general, domestic violence forums have a relatively participatory and collective management system and structure in regard to worker employment, in keeping with wider ideas about equalising power differences between member agencies and evolving collective, coordinated practice and policy responses.** In addition, domestic violence forum employees need to be able to work autonomously but responsibly, to be confident advocates for the forum, to have the ability to 'broker' the inter-agency process, and to be able to negotiate with senior managers and policy makers, as discussed above. In order to secure staff of this calibre, inter-agency projects have tended to adopt participatory managerial systems, although, in one of the study areas, a more traditional, hierarchical management style was in operation.

Summary

■ The majority of forums develop specific *aims and objectives*. They may go on to develop comprehensive *terms of reference*, including *mission statements* and *equal opportunity statements*, which require regular reviewing. Many domestic violence forums do not have constitutions, although some do. Some have become voluntary sector projects, limited companies or charities, while others have remained as networks or as organisations operating under the auspices of one agency.

■ As domestic violence forums become more established, many create a formal structure. Most commonly, this consists of a smaller steering group or steering committee/ management committee to manage the day-to-day running of the initiative. Steering committees need to have an active, committed, representative membership, to be accountable to the full forum and to develop clear procedures and lines of accountability.

■ Many forums establish sub-groups to progress different types of work, which can work particularly well if participation in them is time-limited, with a specific task to accomplish, and with consistency of attendance and commitment from participants. Sub-groups also need to be clear about their remit and their accountability.

■ In order to progress the work, several of the initiatives in the study areas developed overall *action plans*. Some forums carry out *service audits* in which an audit of the work of each member agency is conducted, often leading to the drawing up of individual agency *action plans*.

■ A lack of "thinking strategically" and of evolving longer term *strategic plans* had apparently impeded progress in some areas. Forums need to plan for the future.

■ Since there is a considerable potential for misunderstandings and confusion in multi-agency initiatives, clarity is required about all issues of structure, responsibility and accountability.

■ In order to develop an influential presence locally, forums need to evolve a clear identify and a recognisable local profile. Consistency of attendance and of commitment by member agencies and their officers, and the building of a 'portfolio' of activities, are of key importance in evolving this identity.

■ One of the strengths of domestic violence inter-agency initiatives is often their grass-roots dynamism. However, gaining local influence frequently involves the commitment of senior or policy-making officers within the local authority, the police force, the probation service and other agencies.

■ Many forums contain a mixture of practitioners and policy makers in order to overcome this contradiction. Alternatively, they may remain as grass-roots initiatives but set up special regular meetings or conferences with senior policy-making officers.

■ In some areas, senior level multi-agency strategy-making groups have been established, specifically to evolve local strategy on domestic violence, but sometimes cut off from practitioner, community or refuge networks. Experiments with county level strategy-making forums involving senior officers, with smaller local practitioner forums feeding information into them, have been tried in some counties but have met with limited success so far. However, the development of coordinated planning between agencies and of local or regional strategy across the area in question is clearly to be encouraged.

■ During the study, lack of resources was the single largest factor inhibiting the development of local inter-agency work on domestic violence. Many research respondents pointed to the lack of provision for resources in the 1995 Home Office Inter-agency Circular. The majority of the statutory agencies in the study areas were themselves facing considerable funding cut-backs and contraction of services, and sometimes could not justify involvement in domestic violence forums unless such involvement could be designated as 'core' work.

■ Some statutory agencies attempted to donate resources to their local forum, for example, providing venues, or rotating the forum secretariat between them, but these contributions were becoming less possible due to increasing pressure of other work. Voluntary sector members and refuges were rarely in a position to donate resources.

■ Thus, the vast majority of inter-agency initiatives have no resources at all, apart from what participating agencies can share. Forums which were in receipt of some funding had obtained it from a variety of sources, including various local authority committees, the Police Authority, partnership initiatives, the Home Office Safer Cities Scheme, and other similar sources. However, funding received was invariably short term precipitating regular funding crises.

■ This situation of resource shortage and financial insecurity militates against constructive forward-planning and project development, and, on a general level, makes it more difficult for inter-agency domestic violence initiatives to fulfil their potential.

■ Current best practice is clearly that multi-agency projects should engage actively in attempting to ensure that direct refuge and advocacy services are adequately resourced. Many initiatives make it a priority to facilitate the development and funding of refuges and emergency services.

■ Interviewees pointed out that the provision of direct services, and the development of educative and preventative work and inter-agency coordination, should go hand-in-hand as different sides of the same coin, rather than as competitors. This can only happen with a measure of separate resourcing for inter-agency work.

■ Most forums across the country do not have employees. However, the study accumulated strong evidence from many areas that the employment of a coordinator was of key importance in progressing inter-agency domestic violence work.

■ While a coordinator's role is to support and facilitate the project, rather than to lead it, a worker of this type can give a domestic violence forum focus and direction, and do behind-the-scenes networking to 'oil' the inter-agency process. It can be helpful if the person employed has some experience of Women's Aid and the refuge movement and a background in women's organisations and services.

■ Interview evidence indicates that the employment of a coordinator alone, without any administrative support, is often insufficient to enable the initiative to develop effectively.

■ Employment structures vary for domestic violence forums. For some, the coordinator is a local authority employee, or the post is 'hosted' by the authority. Other inter-agency initiatives are situated in the voluntary sector with a voluntary steering or management committee. In general, domestic violence forums have a relatively participatory management system and structure in regard to worker employment, in keeping with wider ideas about equalising power differences between member agencies and evolving collective, coordinated practice and policy responses.

Chapter 7

Work done by inter-agency initiatives

10. Liaison and networking

10.1 For many inter-agency initiatives, one of their main functions is exchanging information and educating each other about their own work on domestic violence (although some interviewees pointed out that care needs to be taken that the experience and expertise of a few members, for example, refuges, is not used as informal training by others with no acknowledgement of this contribution). Such exchanges of information usually result in better practice. Interviewees throughout the study were almost totally unanimous that networking and communication improved greatly between agencies as a result of inter-agency initiatives. Thus, even where no further coordinating work is attempted, improved networking is of value and benefit in itself (see also Sections **5.1** and **5.2**).

10.2 Some interviewees pointed out that the 'talking shop' aspect of inter-agency work could fulfil a useful function if it concentrated on the needs of women experiencing domestic violence and their children, rather than becoming bogged down in repetitive discussions of process or structures.

10.3 However, some groups which remain only networking groups over a considerable period of time (eg, the original Bristol Domestic Violence Forum), have a tendency to 'run out of steam' and to stop meeting. The North Wales Domestic Violence Forum went through a difficult period when the probation partnership post which was involved with it was coming to an end. In this situation, Welsh Women's Aid took on a major part of the servicing and networking work because other agencies found themselves unable to make the contributions necessary to maintain the initiative. Such situations can place strain on individual agencies and can appear to be a waste of time and energy, when resources are already very scarce. Forums in this type of position may experience an 'identity crisis' and be unclear how to move forward.

10.4 Nevertheless, very many domestic violence forums remain as networking groups throughout their existence. Mapping survey interviews demonstrated that, in some circumstances, this could be as a result of careful, realistic and positive decisions on behalf of the forum and could be a constructive and useful development. Various interviewees pointed out that "knowing who to phone about what" and "being able to put a face to a name" usually improves the coordination of services and the agency responses which women and children experiencing domestic violence receive. Remaining a networking group may be due to lack of time, to member agencies being over-stretched, to lack of resources, to lack of incentive and leadership, to the fact that domestic violence may not be a priority for member agencies and to a variety of other local factors. In the mapping study, groups which were in this position spoke most often of lack of resources and of time as being the major factors governing why they were unable to develop their domestic violence work further.

10.5 Apart from networking and exchanging information, the main work undertaken by inter-agency initiatives comprises:

■ coordinating local services;

■ attempting to improve the practice of agencies and service delivery;

■ engaging in public education, awareness raising and preventative work.

These types of work are discussed in the next section.

11. Carrying on beyond networking – types of work taken on

Coordinating local services

11.1 Coordinating services includes a wide range of activities, many of which are described in later sections. It may include initiating specific and practical improvements in referral systems and collaborative work between agencies. In various areas surveyed, for example, the work of domestic violence forums has led to improved referrals between refuges and the police. Some forums conduct monitoring exercises of domestic violence responses across agencies.

11.2 Coordination may include producing material which enables agencies to work together more effectively. One example is the production of resource directories and guides to improve local liaison. For instance, DDVAG has produced a comprehensive resource directory of domestic violence services for the use of all local agencies, and a number of other forums were doing similar work during the research period (eg, Dorset and North Wales).

12. Attempting to improve local service delivery

12.1 As discussed in **6.14**, many multi-agency initiatives begin work on improving services by conducting a detailed *service audit*. Member agencies and forums themselves audit the work on domestic violence conducted by each agency. A detailed *action plan* can then be drawn up and agreed for each member agency. Inter-agency forums also conduct local research studies to identify particular unmet needs (eg, of disabled women experiencing domestic violence) in order to improve practice (see also Chapter 2, p 10).

12.2 Improving service delivery may include formulating and assisting in implementing general multi-agency practice guidelines to be used by all member agencies. Such guidelines tend to include practice information on how to work with women survivors of domestic violence, on adopting a believing, supportive attitude, on confidentiality, on housing, welfare and legal rights, and on local resources. The London Borough of Islington Women's Equality Unit, in conjunction with Islington Inter-agency Domestic Violence Working Party (see London Borough of Islington, 1992), and other similar initiatives (eg, in other London boroughs) have developed good practice guides for use across the whole local authority in an attempt to contribute to a corporate response. The Leeds Inter-agency Project has developed a range of multi-agency practice materials of this nature. Various study areas had multi-agency practice guidelines in place, although these were sometimes rather short and basic.

12.3 Domestic violence forums may produce specific practice guidance for particular groups of workers. For example, the Islington project has produced a guide specifically for community advisers in the borough.

12.4 Inter-agency initiatives may also work with individual agencies to assist in developing specific domestic violence policies and good practice guidelines. It is now becoming commonly accepted as good practice for statutory agencies to develop such domestic violence policies. Agencies developing policies and practice guidance of this type include the police force, social services departments, the probation service, and housing departments and housing associations (most usually on the implementation of the homelessness legislation in respect of domestic violence) (see also Chapter 8).

12.5 Where a local multi-agency initiative exists, research interviews indicate that it is important that it is fully consulted and involved in the development of policy and practice guidelines by individual agencies. In one of the study areas, for example, a leaflet for internal use within an agency, and, in another, some new practice guidance for another agency, were developed without following consultation procedures. The inter-agency forum did not know of these developments until they were completed. In both cases, the documents produced contained omissions which could have been avoided if the multi-agency project had been involved.

12.6 Research interview material indicated that a considerable amount of liaison work and 'building bridges' may have to occur before an inter-agency forum will be in a position to influence local policy and practice developments. In some of the areas studied, small local forums were often overlooked on a general level when large agencies were evolving domestic violence policy. **In this context, the research generated evidence, as noted, that it could be important for the forum to have the support of higher management in member agencies** (see Section **7** on gaining influence and Chapter 8 on seniority issues in relation to specific agencies).

12.7 In some areas, the domestic violence forum was able to act as an informal 'watchdog' on the quality of services. Effectiveness in this respect generally depended on the local profile of the forum. Some were able to monitor referrals, to take up instances of bad practice with the relevant agency, and, in the words of one interviewee "to keep an eye on what the agencies are doing". This type of practice has been adopted by the Sheffield Domestic Violence Forum. Senior officers from different agencies (eg, social services, the police and probation) have been invited to forum meetings to describe the work of the agency on domestic violence and to be informally 'held accountable' for it.

The Children's Needs Sub-group, which was part of the Cleveland Multi-agency Domestic Violence Forum until the county of Cleveland ceased to exist in 1996, was an innovative development, bringing together representatives of various agencies including children's workers from refuges, specialist children's organisations, such as the Children's Society and the NSPCC, and statutory agencies, in particular, the local authority social services and education departments. The group prepared a report to the local Under-Eight's Committee (a multi-agency committee which was led by Cleveland Social Services and looked at the needs of young children across the area). It participated in a multi-agency task group drawing up new policies on children and domestic violence for the social services department, and Inter-agency Procedures and Practice Guidance commissioned by the local Area Child Protection Committee. It also worked on improving the funding for and provision of children's workers in refuges, and on developing a self-learning pack for children for use in schools, in conjunction with teacher training on the issue.

12.8 While the mapping study indicated that work with children who have witnessed or experienced domestic violence is often overlooked by domestic violence forums, two of the study areas (Greenwich and Cleveland) have developed specific sub-groups to work on children's issues. Such sub-groups may work on a multi-agency basis to evolve policy and practice in relation to children and domestic violence, to take up issues about gaps in services, to provide training and to advocate (in a general way) on behalf of children with other agencies.

13. Initiating domestic violence training for agencies

13.1 Many domestic violence forums design and provide domestic violence training or coordinate its provision by other agencies. Interviewees pointed out that, in doing so, it is important that already existing training work by Women's Aid and others is not duplicated or even, in the words of one interviewee, "hi-jacked" but, rather, that new training initiatives are developed in partnership. It was also pointed out that there needs to be clarity about any payment to be made for delivering training and about who owns any resource material produced.

13.2 Domestic violence training may be delivered to either multi-agency or single agency groups, either as free-standing training units or as part of in-service training programmes. The Domestic Violence Forum in South Bristol, for example, has designed multi-agency training courses, run under the auspices of Bristol Social Services, which are being extended to other areas of the city. Training can usefully be targeted towards specific groups of workers (including managers) and needs to be monitored to gauge its effectiveness and to identify future training needs.

The Leeds Domestic Violence Inter-agency Project has conducted an extensive and detailed training programme in one area of Leeds. Six hundred front-line workers from all the local agencies working in this area have received domestic violence training, using a Training the Trainers model based on ground-breaking training modules developed by the Leeds project. Similarly innovative training was also evolved originally by the Hammersmith and Fulham Domestic Violence Forum. Derivations of this work are widely used, sometimes now offered through a particular domestic violence consultancy firm.

The Derby Domestic Violence Action Group Lifeline is a helpline for anyone experiencing domestic violence and is staffed by volunteers with professional support. The volunteers are offered a thorough initial training programme. Apart from domestic violence awareness and information on services, this incorporates training on all aspects of equalities work, including racism and disability equality. Ongoing training includes further specialist units on living with HIV and AIDS, cultural issues and sexuality. Age issues are also included.

13.3 The mapping survey and the detailed fieldwork yielded evidence that domestic violence forums often deliver training by providing an initial Training the Trainers course usually facilitated by outside consultants, by domestic violence trainers, or by specialists from the Women's Aid federations or from other multi-agency domestic violence groups. Trained officers are then able to deliver further training within their own agencies, or on a multi-agency basis, on a 'cascade' model.

13.4 In several of the study areas, specific training sub-groups or subforums have been set up to coordinate training provision.

13.5 From the evidence of the research study, it appears that domestic violence training usually involves a mixture of awareness-raising and training on specific local policies and practice. It may include the use of innovative training techniques and exercises, including some emphasis on personal and emotional issues and on an analysis of gender inequalities and of power and control issues between men and women. The training material provided by the Duluth Domestic Abuse Intervention Project (see Chapter 2) is particularly popular.

13.6 Current best practice, as described to the research team by trainers, multi-agency workers and members of domestic violence forum training sub-groups, is that equalities issues and the development of anti-discriminatory practice should be integral parts of all training offered, rather than something which is 'added on'.

13.7 In some areas researched (see Section **26**), interviewees felt that, even where a commitment to equal opportunities work within multi-agency training courses had been made, equalities issues were still overlooked; for example, training was not culturally sensitive, did not meet the needs of specific groups of women, such as women from minority ethnic communities or disabled women, or did not take on issues of discrimination (eg, on grounds of class or sexuality).

14. Engaging in public education work

14.1 The research collected evidence that many domestic violence forums produce leaflets, booklets and posters for the public or for women and children experiencing domestic violence.

Most domestic violence forums which have moved beyond being networking groups have produced material of this type and have distributed it.

14.2 Some forums have produced specific information and educational material. For example, the Asian Women's Sub-group of the Greenwich Multi-agency Domestic Violence Forum has produced a publication on the needs of Asian women.

14.3 Few forums, however, involve women who have experienced domestic violence directly in public education work. In Derby, Sunderland and other areas, a start has been made towards incorporating the views of abused women directly into publicity material. In some instances, women who have experienced violence have worked out what should be included in the publicity or have actually written the material. For example, the Sunderland Multi-agency Domestic Violence Forum has produced a leaflet in this way, and women in a local refuge there have also run their own advice line.

14.4 Inter-agency initiatives may engage in other types of public education work, putting on exhibitions about domestic violence or running roadshows, providing stalls at community events or setting up public meetings, workshops, plays etc. In Walsall, for example, a major awareness initiative was held in the central shopping arcade and theatrical events have been staged. In Derby, roadshows have been held with mobile exhibitions of material translated into community languages and large print and on to tape, providing members of the public with the opportunity to engage in discussion. The Nottinghamshire Domestic Violence Forum has produced a travelling exhibition and some forums have made use of Theatre in Education (TIE) to mount performances (eg, Plymouth).

14.5 In common with other aspects of inter-agency practice, not all of these many events followed good equal opportunities practice according to research respondents (see Section **26**). For example, publicity material was not always translated into other languages and on to audio tape, and plays and performances did not always demonstrate awareness of cultural issues.

Zero Tolerance campaigns

14.6 Some inter-agency initiatives have initiated Zero Tolerance campaigns on a multi-agency basis. Such campaigns are most commonly based on the original pioneering campaign run in Edinburgh and are coordinated by local authority officers. Unusually, the Cleveland Multi-agency Domestic Violence Forum is currently coordinating a well-financed Zero Tolerance campaign funded by the local councils, and by the previous Cleveland County Council in particular, but run by the local forum itself. In Bristol, a multi-agency Zero Tolerance campaign was established during the research period, but without the funding to purchase the campaign material produced by Edinburgh Women's Committee. Derby had agreed to run a campaign as the research concluded. Short campaigns were held in the London boroughs before the research commenced. Kirklees, Lancashire and a variety of other areas had developed campaigns during the research period.

14.7 Research evidence from Cleveland and from elsewhere, particularly from the Scottish campaigns, indicates that Zero Tolerance campaigns are usually successful public awareness exercises, at least while they are in operation, and have been received favourably, and often with enthusiasm, by some agencies and by many members of the public. Contention exists, however, as to their effectiveness and durability. Evaluations show that Zero Tolerance needs to be accompanied by community development and education activities, for example, women's self-help and community training courses, which

may be conducted on a multi-agency basis (see Kitzinger and Hunt, 1993).

14.8 The evaluation of the Cleveland campaign indicates that, during its first phase, conducted during the research period, it was successful in terms of recognisability and visibility, although there had been some contentious issues around it. Of the 25 women interviewed in the study in Cleveland, 9 had heard of the campaign and some were very enthusiastic about it, often feeling vindicated in their experiences and excited that an issue which had caused them such great personal pain and trauma was finally being aired. It was perhaps disappointing that 16 women had not heard of the campaign.

14.9 Women interviewed for the research made the point that contact information about local services for women and children experiencing domestic violence needs to be visible on Zero Tolerance campaign material. One interviewee had put herself in considerable personal danger from her violent partner in order to approach a Zero Tolerance poster so that she could secretly memorise contact information from it. This woman lived in sheltered accommodation with her husband and her actions were tightly circumscribed by him. Trying to look at the poster was an act of considerable personal bravery. The woman was extremely upset to find that there was no information on the poster. She did manage to leave months later when she found another source of information, but had been abused many times in-between.

14.10 Where the provision of services is inadequate and projects are crucially under-funded, the research collected evidence, during the mapping study, of difficulty and contention in some areas about the implementation of the campaign. In one area, some agencies had disagreed with some of the campaign poster material. In others, over-stretched projects and refuge groups said that they felt even more over-stretched and burdened by increased demand as a result of a local Zero Tolerance campaign, and sometimes put forward the view that the money could have been better spent on improving existing services rather than further stressing them. The central involvement of refuge services in Zero Tolerance (as in Cleveland, for example) could militate against difficulties of this type arising, although shortage of resources is undoubtedly the strongest factor at work. In Cleveland, the local refuge most involved in the Zero Tolerance campaign is relatively well resourced.

14.11 The counter-argument to this difficulty, which was presented to the researchers, was that the campaign can raise the profile of the issue of violence against women in a locality and can, as a result, facilitate future increases in funding for the services which exist, or for new ones.

15. Establishing direct services for women and children

15.1 There continues to be a need for independent advice and support for abused women and children which is not linked to statutory responsibilities. Night telephone lines and other information lines and services have been set up by various domestic violence forums. In 1995, DDVAG, for example, established the DDVAG Lifeline, a night helpline for anyone experiencing violence. The Lifeline is staffed by volunteers for limited hours. The volunteers have received comprehensive initial and ongoing training and supervision, as described in Section **13**. For each session, at least one of the volunteers on duty can speak a number of locally-used community languages.

15.2 Inter-agency initiatives have also established self-help groups and drop-in sessions for abused women and children. For example, one of the local

forums in Bristol, the Lawrence Weston Domestic Violence Forum, has established a successful survivors support group. The Cleveland Multi-agency Forum has also set up women's support groups of domestic violence survivors in each of its four districts and is planning to set up a one-stop advice centre for abused women and children with all the services coordinated under one roof.

15.3 Multi-agency initiatives to set up new projects of this type can be highly successful (especially if linked in with existing women's services) in that work is shared, and a joint initiative is undertaken which one agency alone could not attempt. They are relatively rare, however, as inter-agency work tends to concentrate on indirect preventative and education work and on coordinating and improving existing services and agency practice. Domestic violence forums can also assist in ensuring that domestic violence is not overlooked in the work of new or existing projects with a wider remit.

16. Educative and preventative projects

16.1 Interviewees from a variety of agencies pointed out that preventative work is conducted directly with abused women and children by refuges (Barron, Harwin and Singh, 1992), even though this aspect of their work is not always recognised. **As discussed in Section 8, many inter-agency projects make it a priority to facilitate increased funding for direct services for women and children, including refuge provision, women's advocacy and support services, and outreach work.** By assisting in increasing emergency provision in this way, they are taking an active role in prevention. In addition, many of the projects (mentioned in Section **15**), which are set up directly by domestic violence forums also have a preventative function in themselves.

Preventative work in the education system

16.2 There is a growing trend for multi-agency initiatives to undertake preventative work in school and youth projects. This may involve the development of comprehensive education packs for use with children in schools, to be accompanied by in-service training for teachers.

16.3 Particularly interesting education projects have been developed by the inter-agency projects in Islington, Leeds and Keighley, where support work in schools has been accompanied by the development of teaching packs and training modules and by youth education work in youth clubs. In Leeds, a support worker was employed by the Inter-agency Project, initially as part of a three-year project funded by the Home Office Programme Development Unit, to develop education programmes for primary schools and to work alongside teachers to test them out in the classroom. In Keighley, a similarly funded programme has developed a resource pack on gender issues and family violence for schools and youth clubs, accompanied by training for teachers and youth and community workers. In addition, the Keighley Domestic Violence Forum has developed an innovative support group for the children of women who have experienced domestic violence, named AWAKENS. In a few cases, forums have developed workshop productions and plays on domestic violence for schools and youth groups.

16.4 Education packs for use in schools have also been developed in various other areas. A few random examples are Kingston-on-Thames, the former Central Region in Scotland (by the Violence Against Women and Children Project in Bannockburn), and Cleveland (through the work of the Children's Needs Sub-group). Also in Cleveland, a multi-agency initiative has developed a group programme for children who have witnessed incidents of domestic violence. The groups have been run jointly by the NSPCC and by the social services department through the Cleveland and Durham Child Protection Team. In Sutton, the original material for an educational programme on domestic violence was written by women sixth-formers for their own school and has now been used in other schools. The Rugby Domestic Violence Project has developed a series of problem-solving workshops for use with children in schools. In Wolver-hampton, the Borough Council has adopted resource material on domestic violence for secondary schools and has made use of youth plays and workshops. Various other inter-agency projects have developed similar education packs and projects.

In 1995, the Islington Women's Equality Unit, in conjunction with the Islington Inter-agency Domestic Violence Working Party and the Islington Education Department, developed and published a comprehensive manual on domestic violence for use in schools. Named *Stop domestic violence*, it includes advice and information for schools and teachers, training modules for teacher training, and extensive curriculum material, exercises, workshop programmes and awareness raising ideas for use in the classroom situation.

Programmes for male perpetrators of domestic violence

16.5 Many perpetrators programmes are now being set up throughout the country. These programmes work with male abusers to attempt to deal with the domestic violence which they have committed, and to address the nature, cause and consequences of their abusive behaviour. Participants attend sessions over a period of weeks and generally make a contract with the programme to remain non-violent throughout the programme. Usually, perpetrators programmes are connected to the probation service, although some are voluntary sector projects which take voluntary referrals, and some are a mixture of both. **Some inter-agency projects are involved in this work.** The Derby IMPACT project, for example, is part of DDVAG and is run directly by the inter-agency project. This project has connections with national networks of male practitioners working with male perpetrators and is committed to working closely with the women's projects dealing with domestic violence in the locality, to taking guidance from them, and to using the Duluth model for understanding domestic violence. As noted in Chapter 2, this model is based on an analysis of power and control in abusive relationships between men and women.

16.6 The Cleveland Multi-agency Forum also runs male perpetrators groups as an integral part of the inter-agency initiative, and, in addition, both the Derby and Cleveland projects run women's support groups alongside the perpetrators programmes. Walsall has obtained funding to run a group for perpetrators. Abusers groups also operate within some of the policy and practice profile areas, but are not run directly by the domestic violence forums. The Greenwich Domestic Violence Forum runs a Working with Men Sub-group.

16.7 **Probation officers tend to be involved in running perpetrators programmes, and partnership funding through probation had been made available to the inter-agency initiatives in both Derby and Cleveland.** Probation officers and project coordinators who were interviewed for the study suggested that current best practice in this context is that perpetrators projects may work best where men are court-mandated (eg, as a condition of their probation order), although disagreement exists about this, in that voluntary referrals may have more personal motivation. Interviewees further discussed best practice in terms of perpetrators programmes avoiding competition for funding with services for abused women and children, and the desirability of some sort of management involvement by local women's projects. They also pointed out that the setting up of 'sister' women's support projects (as noted above), which may be independently run, is accepted as good practice, and that a 'pro-feminist' programme like the Duluth model, is most applicable. (Pro-feminist abusers programmes are explained further in Adams, 1988; Hague and Malos, 1993.) Contention continues to exist, however, about the efficacy of these projects on any level as a remedy for men's violence against women.

Summary

■   Many inter-agency projects are networking groups in which member agencies exchange information and educate each other. Networking of this type has value in itself. Some interviewees pointed out that the 'talking shop' aspect of inter-agency work could fulfil a useful function if it concentrated on the needs of women experiencing domestic violence and their children, rather than becoming bogged down in repetitive discussions of process and structures. However, some initiatives had lost their momentum due to remaining networking groups. Lack of time and resources often inhibited groups from moving on to other work.

■ Apart from networking, the main work of inter-agency initiatives comprises: coordinating local services; attempting to improve agency practice and service delivery; and engaging in public education, awareness raising and preventative work.

■ Coordinating services includes a wide range of activities including initiating specific improvements in practice between agencies, producing material which enables agencies to work together more effectively, and conducting monitoring and research.

■ Improving service delivery may include formulating and assisting in implementing general multi-agency practice guidelines to be used by all member agencies, or practice guidance for particular groups of workers. Inter-agency initiatives may also work with individual agencies to conduct *service audits* and to develop specific domestic violence policies and good practice guidelines for each agency. Where a local multi-agency initiative exists, it is important that it is fully consulted and involved in the development of policy and practice guidelines.

■ A considerable amount of liaison work and 'building bridges' may have to occur before an inter-agency forum is in a position to influence local policy and practice developments, and the support of higher management in member agencies is essential in this endeavour.

■ While the mapping study indicated that work with children who have witnessed or experienced domestic violence is often overlooked by domestic violence forums, two of the study areas have developed specific sub-groups to work on children's issues.

■ Many domestic violence forums establish Training Sub-groups, and coordinate the design and provision of domestic violence training, sometimes in partnership with Women's Aid. There needs to be clarity about who owns any training resources produced and about any payment made for delivering training. Training programmes usually involve a mixture of awareness-raising and training on specific local policies and practice, often delivered on a 'cascade' Training the Trainers model.

■ Best practice is that equalities issues and the development of anti-discriminatory practice should be integral parts of all training offered, rather than something which is 'added on' as an extra feature.

■ Many domestic violence forums produce leaflets, booklets and posters for the public or for women and children experiencing domestic violence. Few forums, however, involve women who have experienced domestic violence directly in public education work.

■ Inter-agency initiatives may also engage in other types of public education work, putting on exhibitions about domestic violence, plays, public meetings, workshops, etc. Some inter-agency initiatives have initiated Zero Tolerance campaigns on a multi-agency basis.

■ Preventative work includes improving facilities for women and children escaping domestic violence, and good practice is that multi-agency initiatives should attempt as a priority to facilitate the development and resourcing of refuges and other emergency services. Some inter-agency forums set up new projects (eg, support groups and helplines).

■ There is a growing trend for multi-agency initiatives to undertake preventative work in school and youth projects. This may involve the development of education packs for use with children in schools to be accompanied by in-service training for teachers.

■ Many perpetrators programmes are now being set up throughout the country. These programmes work with male abusers to attempt to deal with the domestic violence which they have committed, and to address the nature, cause and consequences of their abusive behaviour. Some inter-agency projects are involved in this work, often in partnership with probation.

Chapter 8

The participation of the statutory sector, Victim Support and national voluntary organisations

17.1 Table 2 (p 53) gives an indication of the relative participation of different agencies in inter-agency domestic violence work currently. The evidence from this study indicates that the police and refuge services are the agencies most often involved. Probation, social services and housing are involved significantly less frequently. Of the statutory agencies, other criminal justice services, local authority education departments and health services participate considerably less frequently again.

17.2 For multi-agency responses to be effective, it was clear from the research both that officers from the relevant statutory services need to be delegated to attend as part of agreed job specifications, and that commitment from managers and policy makers is essential. However, there were difficulties in both these respects in various study areas, as discussed below.

17. The involvement of the police

17.3 As noted, the police have taken a very active role in many domestic violence forums in recent years. Evidence from the mapping study suggests that police forces are more involved than they were when the Home Office study discussed in Chapter 2 was conducted

(Grace, 1995). While interview evidence described some difficulties where forums were dominated by the police (as noted in Section **3**), and wider philosophical and 'political' issues can be debated about the involvement of the police and the refuge movement in joint work (see Chapter 2), police inter-agency work on domestic violence has often been conducted sensitively, according to research interviews.

17.4 In one of the study areas, the local constabulary had deliberately taken a background role, but officers had then felt frustrated on occasion at the slow rate of change. The phenomenon of the police taking a less active role than they feel capable of, in order to avoid dominating proceedings, has also been noted in other multi-agency arenas (Liddle and Gelsthorpe, 1994b, p 12).

17.5 On the other hand, as noted, some problems could be experienced, according to research respondents, when the police took a very active initiating and leading role within inter-agency domestic violence initiatives. In general, the interviews offered tentative evidence that such problems were fewer where police domestic violence units or dedicated domestic violence officer posts were in existence (as in Walsall and Dorset). Interviewees indicated that domestic violence forums which were always chaired and dominated by police officers could experience difficulties, as could forums which routinely met in the local police station (in that some agencies were not comfortable in using that venue).

Table 2: Active participation of agencies in domestic violence inter-agency initiatives (50 randomly chosen domestic violence forums from the mapping study)

Agency	Number of forums participated in
Police	43
Refuges	40
Local authority special units (where these existed)	18
Local authority housing departments	27
Local authority social services departments	28
Local authority education departments	6
Probation	26
Legal/Court personnel	5
CPS	5
Solicitors	14
Health services	13
Victim Support	21
Voluntary sector/ charities/women's community groups	24

17.6 In most of the study areas, the police were involved at both practitioner and policy-making levels, and the support of the Chief Constable had been obtained in several cases (eg, Cleveland). In general, policy-making and senior officers appeared to be more committed to, and in some cases more involved in, inter-agency domestic violence initiatives than senior managers in other agencies. While this differential level of involvement may result from the relevant Home Office guidance on the issue (as discussed in Chapters 1 and 2), it was clear from the study interviews in a variety of locations that the police commitment could be a demonstration of good practice in this respect. It appeared from the research evidence that the active support of senior officers was extremely helpful and could have a transforming effect on police involvement.

17.7 In the West Midlands, all the domestic violence forums had been set up by the police. A police inspector with particular responsibility for domestic violence across the area worked with all the local forums and domestic violence units. The Walsall Forum was part of this arrangement. The police had been very active in establishing it and, in the past, had provided both the chair and some of the secretarial and administrative work.

17.8 In South Yorkshire, the Police Authority had made domestic violence a funding priority during the research period. It had funded both the employment of two inter-agency domestic violence co-ordinators, working with the Sheffield Forum, and the coordinating work performed by the South Yorkshire Working Group. Also during the research period, Cleveland Constabulary played an active and important part in promoting and supporting both the Cleveland Multi-agency Forum and the Zero Tolerance campaign. In Dorset, the police domestic violence officers have taken a key role in developing the domestic violence forum, including the organisation of a major regional conference. Interviewees in Dorset pointed out that the inter-agency initiative would not have taken off without this police investment and were very positive about the work of the police domestic violence coordinator. She was, one interviewee said "not like you expect a police officer to be".

17.9 In many areas investigated, the police had developed policy and practice guidance on domestic violence and had produced publicity material. As noted previously, research interviews suggested that these developments had sometimes occurred without the full participation of the local domestic violence forum. In one of the study areas, however, new force guidance had been consulted fully with the forum and, in another, police representatives meet regularly with representatives of the forum (outside forum meetings) to discuss and monitor police practice.

17.10 Nevertheless, while harmonious relations within domestic violence forums appear to exist in many areas surveyed during the research, it is also clear from research interviews that difficulties can be experienced between the police and some agencies participating in inter-agency work.

17.11 Research interviews suggest that many agencies have doubts about the extent and depth of real change in recent domestic violence policing, and both the social control function of the police force and also its masculine ethos have led many women's groups to voice concern about building close liaisons. Some views were also expressed by grass-roots organisations that co-operation with the police is inappropriate while more aggressive policing practices continue to exist in relation to certain groups. In particular, accusations of racism in a number of police forces, and the policing of the immigration legislation, have led many black women's groups to view inter-agency liaison with suspicion (as briefly discussed in Chapter 2). A large number of our research informants, including police officers themselves, were clear about the crucial role played by the police in domestic violence inter-agency work, but still did not wish to diminish or under-estimate the difficulties thrown up by police involvement.

18. The involvement of the probation service, the courts and the legal services

18.1 The Association of Chief Officers of Probation (ACOP) issued an important *Position statement on domestic violence* in 1992, updated in 1996, which has been widely welcomed by refuges and by domestic violence practitioners. In addition, a National Association of Probation Officers (NAPO) working party is currently drafting a statement on domestic violence to include standards on perpetrators projects, for NAPO members. The Home Affairs Committee (1993) identified the probation service as a key agency in domestic violence work. Within this developing interest, the participation of probation in inter-agency responses is often seen as a helpful contribution.

18.2 As a result, the probation service takes an active role in some inter-agency initiatives, often through involvement with perpetrators groups as discussed in Section **16.5-16.7**, or sometimes through the Court Welfare Service. The study provided evidence that individual probation officers often attend domestic violence forums, reporting back to their colleagues on domestic violence issues, and vice versa.

18.3 In some areas, senior probation officers are involved in joint multi-agency groups with other senior policy makers to evolve a coordinated local domestic violence strategy (see also Section **7**). Research interviews indicated that chief officer and senior management involvement in developing wider strategy of this type could greatly improve coordinated local service delivery and that the development is to be recommended, with some reservations.

18.4 In other cases, however, the involvement of the probation service in domestic violence forums may occur almost in spite of, rather than because of, the agency. It may then depend on the individual enthusiasm of particular officers, often, although not always, women, who may also struggle to get domestic violence taken seriously by their colleagues.

18.5 Probation services in various areas have developed, or are developing, new practice guidelines on domestic violence to improve the service offered by officers. The research indicates that, where local forums exist, the development of practice guidance of this type usually involves consultation with the forum, and that this consultation is to be recommended. The research also identified areas where probation officers had participated in multi-agency task groups to draw up and implement domestic violence policies and practice guidelines across agencies or to develop specific guidance on a particular area of work in relation to domestic violence, for example, child protection. (For a further discussion of multi-agency domestic violence work in relation to the probation service, see Hague, Malos and Dear, 1995b.)

18.6 As noted in Section **4**, the CPS, court personnel, judges and magistrates were rarely active in inter-agency domestic violence initiatives during the study period. Some domestic violence forums, however, are developing training packages for magistrates and court officers. Projects to support abused women using the criminal justice system have been established by a few forums. For example, the Civil and Criminal Justice Project of the Leeds Inter-agency Forum (which had financial support from the Home Office Programme Development Unit between 1993 and 1996) is involved in a variety of activities including training and a volunteer support scheme for abused women, named the HALT project.

18.7 During the research private solicitors firms were more often represented on local domestic violence forums. In Derby, for example, a solicitors

firm was strongly represented on the management committee and the training sub-committee. In some areas (eg, West Sussex and one of the Bristol forums), local solicitors have taken a leading role in establishing the inter-agency initiative.

19. The involvement of social services departments

19.1 Social services have a crucial role to play in meeting the needs of women and children experiencing domestic violence. Social services departments are active in a large number of domestic violence forums. However, the mapping study also showed that social services are absent surprisingly often, given their fundamental importance in domestic violence work. In many instances, the research revealed that the domestic violence forum may be attended by a basic grade social worker on an ad hoc basis or out of personal interest, with little or no support from managers or from others in the department. In a few localities investigated during the study (including Dorset, Walsall, Cleveland and Greenwich), area team managers were involved, but in general, policy makers and social services management were not in evidence. Representatives from several forums expressed disappointment at this situation and pointed out the need for commitment to the work from senior management.

19.2 This lack of active commitment in some areas may reflect the increasing pressure of social workers' time. It may also reflect the lack of priority accorded to domestic violence within many teams despite recent improvements (see Mullender, forthcoming; Farmer and Owen, 1993). As in the case of the police and the probation service, where a departmental and policy commitment existed, social workers in the study were able to take a more active and creative role in the inter-agency work done, to the mutual benefit of both the department and the domestic violence forum.

19.3 The connections between child abuse and domestic violence, and also the effects on children of witnessing and experiencing domestic violence, are issues which have increasingly engaged social workers in the last few years. With input from the Women's Aid movement, there have been many conferences and seminars on the subject of children and domestic violence, together with publications (eg, Mullender and Morley, 1994); and research studies (National Children's Homes, 1994; Hague et al, 1996; Hester and Radford, 1996). These developments have led to a greater involvement of social services departments in inter-agency forums and in children's work within these in particular (see Section **12**).

19.4 Domestic violence now features in many community care and children's services plans, often with the involvement of multi-agency task groups. Wherever this was the case, interviewees expressed support and encouragement for the resulting initiatives.

19.5 Some social services departments have developed domestic violence policies and good practice guidance, in consultation with their local domestic violence forum.

19.6 The inter-agency approach was one of the issues highlighted by two Social Services Inspectorate/DoH Seminars in 1995 (Ball, 1996). **The study indicated that further local and national guidance encouraging social services departments to participate in multi-agency work on domestic violence would be welcome.**

20. The involvement of housing departments and associations and the education service

20.1 Housing departments are often active in multi-agency domestic violence forums, most usually through the participation of their homelessness section or homeless persons unit. It is to this section or unit that women and children who are homeless due to domestic violence most frequently turn. One of the foremost needs of women and children in this situation is for safe permanent accommodation of a decent standard (see Malos and Hague, 1993). **Thus housing departments and other housing bodies play a crucial role in responding to domestic violence. Sometimes housing managers are involved in inter-agency initiatives, and sometimes housing officers.** In several areas studied, housing managers supported the domestic violence initiative in an active way, and had been involved in evolving housing policy on domestic violence. However, in many others, housing involvement and support from housing management was absent.

20.2 The involvement of housing bodies in multi-agency domestic violence initiatives sometimes takes the form of work with other agencies in multi-agency groups to evolve domestic violence policy and practice in terms of housing. The Greenwich Fightback group, for example, involving the housing department and local refuges, has developed a new housing policy and relevant training modules for housing officers.

20.3 In Bristol, the City Council Housing Department developed a domestic violence and homelessness policy, adopted in 1993. The Housing Department was simultaneously involved in launching the first Bristol Domestic Violence Forum.

20.4 As for other statutory agencies, further local and national guidance on participation in multi-agency domestic violence initiatives would be of benefit.

20.5 As discussed in **16.2-16.4**, local authority education departments are sometimes involved in working with inter-agency forums, or in multi-agency working parties, to evolve education packs and training on domestic violence. **In general, however, education departments are rarely active in domestic violence forums.**

21. The involvement of health services

21.1 Health visitors and representatives of Accident and Emergency departments from health trusts are quite active in inter-agency work in a few areas. In general, however, it appears from the results of the mapping study that health authorities and health trust professionals are not much involved in many inter-agency initiatives. Doctors and other primary care health staff, with the exception of midwives and health visitors in some areas, are noted by their absence. Multi-agency work on domestic violence features in various community care plans (see **19.4**).

21.2 Where local health services were involved in multi-agency domestic violence work in the study, this involvement was much appreciated by both practitioners and policy makers from other agencies. **Interviewees in many areas wished to strongly encourage health services to become more actively involved in this work.** Due to the vital importance of health care for women experiencing domestic violence and their children, the absence of health professionals from the majority of domestic violence forums was much regretted. **National and local**

guidance on this issue is urgently needed and would be broadly welcomed. **The importance of improving the extent and level of participation by health services in multi-agency domestic violence work cannot be over-emphasised.**

22. The involvement of Victim Support

22.1 Nationally, Victim Support has been pro-active in encouraging the establishment of inter-agency work (National Inter-Agency Working Party Report, 1992), and local groups frequently participate in domestic violence forums, as noted. Victim Support groups may play a leading role in setting up forums and in the development of comprehensive support services.

22.2 While several forums contacted during the mapping study had been initiated by Victim Support groups, the local groups in most of the study areas were not notably active or involved in the inter-agency initiative in those areas. Commonly, this lack of involvement was described as being due to overwork. In Walsall, however, Victim Support were referred to by several agencies as the "linchpin of the forum", and had done a great deal of work to facilitate and develop it. Victim Support was also actively involved in the steering group of the Dorset Forum.

23. The involvement of national voluntary organisations

23.1 As national organisations, the Women's Aid federations have played a key role in developing and encouraging multi-agency initiatives, both at national policy level and in relation to particular initiatives, such as Dorset and North Wales. WAFE has been particularly active in providing consultancy and training on inter-agency development (see Section **25**).

23.2 The local bodies of some national voluntary organisations (eg, Relate, NSPCC, National Federation of Housing Association, Citizens' Advice Bureaux) participate in some inter-agency forums.

23.3 National voluntary organisations may wish to take on the issue of domestic violence to a greater extent in the future, and consider what part they could best play in local initiatives. (Victim Support has been particularly active nationally as noted in the preceding section.) Guidance from national organisations for local member groups on participation in multi-agency domestic violence work would be of assistance.

Summary

■ For multi-agency responses to be effective, officers from the relevant statutory agencies need to be delegated to attend as part of agreed job specifications, and commitment from managers and policy makers is essential. However, there were difficulties in both respects in various study areas.

■ The police have taken a very active role in many domestic violence forums in recent years. Inter-agency work on domestic violence by the police has often been conducted sensitively with a very considerable police input in terms of time, commitment and resources. On the other hand, some problems could be experienced, according to research respondents, when the police took a very active initiating and leading role, or dominated the proceedings, when police officers always took the chair or when the forum met in police premises. These problems were usually less pronounced where police domestic violence units or dedicated domestic violence officer posts were in existence.

■ In most of the study areas, the police were involved at both practitioner and policy-making levels, and the support of the Chief Constable had been obtained in several cases. In general, policy-making and senior officers appeared to be substantially more committed to inter-agency domestic violence initiatives than senior managers in other agencies. In several areas investigated, the police had developed policy and practice guidance on domestic violence and had produced publicity material.

■ Nevertheless, while harmonious relations within domestic violence forums appear to exist in many areas, it is also clear that difficulties can be experienced between the police and some agencies participating in inter-agency work, in terms of doubts about the extent and depth of real change in recent domestic violence policing. Doubts were also expressed about the social control function of the police force, its masculine ethos, and aggressive or potentially racist policing practices in relation to certain groups, which could influence the effectiveness of inter-agency cooperation.

■ The probation service takes an active role in some inter-agency initiatives, often through involvement with perpetrators groups (or sometimes through the Court Welfare Service). Individual probation officers often attend domestic violence forums, and in some areas, senior probation officers are involved in joint multi-agency groups with other senior policy makers to evolve a coordinated local domestic violence strategy.

■ Probation services in various areas have developed new practice guidelines on domestic violence to improve the service offered by officers. In other cases, however, the involvement of the probation service in inter-agency forums and in other domestic violence work may occur almost in spite of, rather than because of, the agency. Further local and national guidance on this issue would be useful.

■ The CPS, court personnel, judges and magistrates are rarely active in inter-agency domestic violence initiatives although a few domestic violence forums have developed training packages for magistrates and court officers, and have initiated projects to support abused women using the criminal justice system. Private solicitors firms are more often active in local domestic violence forums and in some cases take a leading role.

■ Social services have a crucial part to play in meeting the needs of women and children experiencing domestic violence, and are active in many domestic violence forums. However, the mapping study also showed that social services are absent surprisingly often, and that support from policy makers and social services management was frequently lacking. As in the case of the police and the probation service, where a departmental and policy commitment existed social workers in the study were able to take a more active and creative role in the inter-agency work done, to the mutual benefit of both the department and the domestic violence forum.

■ Domestic violence now features in many community care and children's services plans, often with the involvement of multi-agency task groups. Some social services departments have developed domestic violence policies and good practice guidance, in consultation with their local domestic violence forum. The study indicated that further local and national guidance encouraging social services departments to participate in multi-agency work on domestic violence would be welcome.

■ Housing authorities and housing associations play a crucial role in responding to domestic violence, and housing departments are frequently active in multi-agency forums, and may have developed domestic violence training and policy initiatives. However, support from housing management is often absent, and further local and national guidance on the involvement of local housing authorities and other housing bodies in inter-agency initiatives would be helpful.

■ Local authority education departments are rarely active in domestic violence forums, except where multi-agency projects to develop education packs are in place, and their greater involvement would be welcomed in most areas.

■ While some health service practitioners and policy makers are quite active in inter-agency work in a few areas, doctors and other primary health care staff are noted by their absence. Due to the vital importance of health care for women experiencing domestic violence and their children, the low rate of involvement of health professionals is a matter of considerable concern. National and local guidance on this issue is urgently needed. The importance of improving the extent and level of participation by health services in multi-agency domestic violence work cannot be over-emphasised.

■ Nationally, Victim Support is pro-active in encouraging the establishment of inter-agency work on domestic violence. Local groups are encouraged to take part and frequently contribute to, and sometimes initiate, domestic violence forums.

■ Representatives from national voluntary organisations participate in some inter-agency forums. Guidance for member groups from national bodies on participation in this work would be of assistance. The national Women's Aid federations offer consultancy, support and training on multi-agency domestic violence work.

Chapter 9

The voluntary sector, Women's Aid and equality issues

24. The involvement of voluntary sector agencies and community groups

24.1 While local voluntary sector groups are represented in most inter-agency domestic violence forums, in some they are not. From the mapping study, it could be seen that this was most often the case where few voluntary organisations existed, where there was no local refuge, or where the initiative was principally a local authority one in terms of building a corporate response to domestic violence across that authority. The study interviews provided evidence, however, that the participation of voluntary sector agencies is vital in achieving inter-agency coordination, since many of the agencies dealing with domestic violence, and refuges in particular, are not statutory or national bodies, although some are affiliated to the national Women's Aid federations or other national organisations.

24.2 Even where there is some involvement, the voluntary sector in general appears to be frequently under-represented on multi-agency forums, and on their steering groups in particular, so that membership may appear skewed towards the statutory sector. Leaving aside refuges, this was the case in the majority of the study areas. In most of these localities, active attempts had been conducted to recruit more voluntary sector members. Resourcing difficulties often militated against agencies becoming involved or making a priority of the work, even when they might have liked to have done so. However, the research showed that voluntary sector agencies need to make a recognisable commitment to the multi-agency process, to 'sign up' to it.

24.3 It was also the case that power differences between statutory and voluntary agencies played a role in deterring some voluntary organisations from taking part.

> "In the forum, there are problems about power – the already powerful groups trying to take control – paralleling the process of abuse – the watchword is 'co-operation' not 'competition'. There is a parallel process in the committee in terms of working with domestic violence – a lot of power play between agencies – mirroring what often happens in a relationship." (Agency interviewee, main study area)

24.4 Some community groups, for example, small women's organisations, including black women's organisations or campaigning groups, felt excluded from the inter-agency initiatives to some extent in almost all the study areas, and many felt inhibited from participating actively. Some voluntary sector interviewees from different areas stated one or several of the following: that they regarded their local forum as an institutional and statutory body; that it appeared to be a white middle class organisation not concerned with issues of equal opportunities; that voluntary sector agencies were not listened to; or that formal or stilted ways of conducting meetings were alienating and inhibiting (as noted in Section **5**). Multi-agency forums may wish to take note of these difficulties and attempt actively to address them.

24.5 These issues of power differences and marginalisation are of most concern in the case of Women's Aid and the refuge movement and they are more fully discussed in the next section.

25. The participation of Women's Aid and the refuge movement

25.1 The central focus of multi-agency work is to improve services for abused women and children and to prevent or reduce the incidence of domestic violence. While Women's Aid is accepted as the lead specialist agency in dealing with domestic violence in both these respects, the Women's Aid federations and refuge groups are, in fact, small organisations, often under-funded, with little realistic power. Interviewees in various areas pointed out, however, that, in the words of one respondent:

> "Women's Aid doesn't have the power like statutory agencies have, but it's the *moral* power they've got." (Agency interviewee, Greenwich)

25.2 As noted in Section 5, one of the most pressing difficulties faced by inter-agency projects can be how to equalise power differences between member agencies and how to maintain the central position of the refuge movement as more objectively powerful agencies, such as the police and the local authority, become involved in

multi-agency coordination. Interviewees in a variety of research locations described how there can be a tendency for the statutory agencies to 'take over' inter-agency work. This may happen not necessarily by intent but due to habits of work, agency attitudes, statutory working practices and differential levels of power and influence. Traditional hostilities and rivalries between the voluntary and the statutory sectors can also play a part here, as pointed out by respondents from both types of agency. When the statutory agencies start to 'own' the issue, in this way, the research demonstrated that there can be a tendency for Women's Aid and other refuges and women's advocacy services to be marginalised within inter-agency work.

25.3 Even where a commitment to the full involvement of refuges exists, however, their full participation is not always possible due to the continual crisis work which they undertake and, frequently, their poor staffing ratios and low pay. Many refuges may have only one or two paid workers. Almost all are in a financial position where they have to use volunteers for some work (eg, answering the phones, operating helplines and support services and, in many refuges, providing children's services), and some depend totally on volunteers. Refuges themselves are in short supply and vacancies for residents are rare. The level of refuge provision proposed by the Select Committee on Violence in Marriage (Parliamentary Select Committee, 1975) has been less than one third met today, after 20 years, and there is evidence that specialist refuges for black women and women from minority ethnic communities are even more severely under-funded (Hague and Malos, 1993; Mama, 1989; Barron, Harwin and Singh, 1992; Russell, 1989). Thus, meaningful involvement by refuges in inter-agency work can appear as an unachievable luxury. Many do what they can, but consistent attendance at regular inter-agency meetings, and the undertaking of projects on behalf of the multi-agency initiative, may be impossible, given the crisis nature of refuge work.

25.4 A large number of research informants pointed out that for multi-agency initiatives to proceed without Women's Aid or refuge involvement makes a nonsense of effective inter-agency coordination. However, it appears from the mapping study that in some extreme cases, refuges are not involved on any level in their local domestic violence forum, or only attend very rarely so that they are unable to follow developments. Some Women's Aid groups contacted during the mapping study wished to participate in local multi-agency work but felt excluded and overlooked by other agencies. **In some areas, it was clear from research interviews that refuges were regarded as just one voluntary agency among many involved in dealing with domestic violence, instead of as the leading specialist organisation in service provision.**

25.5 Inter-agency projects have used various techniques to overcome these difficulties. **An approach practised within two of the main study research areas, and elsewhere, is for local refuges to take a major role within the multi-agency initiative as an agreed principle of its operation.** One possibility is for Women's Aid or other local refuges to take a formal and visible role. **In some areas, Women's Aid takes the chair of the organisation, although statutory agencies with more resources may agree to take on a larger share of the organisational or administrative work to relieve Women's Aid of these duties.** In others, a statutory agency does the work of chairing since voluntary sector organisations may not have the resources to do so. However, Women's Aid may take a central role in other ways. **For example, a reserved place on the steering committee may be delegated to Women's Aid as an agreed principle of the organisation.**

25.6 In Derby, local refuges take a very active part in the work of DDVAG. While examples of the tendency of statutory organisations to attempt to 'own' the issue can be detected in the Derby project, as elsewhere, and tensions are sometimes experienced between powerful statutory agencies and small voluntary organisations like refuges, a positive attitude has been adopted.

Factors influencing the positive involvement of refuges in DDVAG:

■   The high priority given to inter-agency coordination by the voluntary sector refuges including the Hadhari Nari Project which runs the Women's Aid refuges in the city of Derby. Other refuge groups are also actively involved.

■   The commitment of statutory agencies within DDVAG to recognising the expertise of Hadhari Nari and other refuges and to working closely together, even when this means challenging and changing their own practice and procedures.

■   The situation of the DDVAG project within the voluntary sector rather than within, or associated with, one particular statutory agency.

■   The principled commitment of DDVAG to the chair of the management committee and the organisation being provided by Hadhari Nari.

25.7 Within DDVAG, Women's Aid itself has an influential voice. As a matter of agreed policy, Hadhari Nari takes the chair of the management committee. However, it was pointed out to the researchers that such extensive involvement takes time and energy away from other work and is only made possible due to the strong commitment of the Hadhari Nari Project to DDVAG. In addition, the officer who chairs DDVAG is the project manager and only works directly in the refuges themselves for a part of her workload. Thus, the Derby experience is not necessarily directly transferable to other refuges and inter-agency projects, where refuge workers may be less able to dedicate time to inter-agency work due to the crisis demands of their continual direct work with abused women and children.

25.8 In general, however, the central involvement of local refuge services in inter-agency work is of crucial importance to allow the voices of Women's Aid, and of women and children experiencing domestic violence, including black women and children, to be heard. Interviewees in a variety of localities, including Derby, Bristol, South Yorkshire and Greenwich, pointed out that it can be a constant struggle for these voices to be heard in a meaningful way. **It can also be an isolating experience when only one or two representatives from refuges are involved in an inter-agency initiative, and have to continually push for their views and for the views of abused women to be taken seriously. Refuge interviewees spoke of sometimes feeling like "lone trouble-makers" as they attempt to raise the interests of women and children experiencing violence in an empowering way.**

25.9 In Cleveland, various refuge groups are involved in inter-agency work. Middlesbrough Women's Aid takes a powerful role in the local multi-agency forum and chairs the general forum meetings. The staff members concerned work directly in the refuge and their involvement is only possible through the cooperation of the entire refuge staff team, particularly those workers who undertake extra duties to cover for those engaged in inter-agency work. A further point was made that two Women's Aid workers may need to be released for this work, if one is in the chair, so that the other can represent the organisation.

25.10 While some participants interviewed for the study expressed some doubts about the strength of Women's Aid position within the Cleveland Forum, and about some of the views and attitudes which the Women's Aid representatives have on occasion expressed, the majority view was that the forum had developed its own particular beliefs and views by working together as a group over a relatively long time. Interviewees were almost unanimous that, as part of this evolution, the opinions and contributions of Women's Aid had played a vital part, and that it was essential that the refuge continued to play a central role since:

> "... they are the experts and the only specialists in domestic violence work. It's only right that they should be in the lead."

> "Women's Aid have been instrumental in holding the forum together and injecting life into it."
> (Interviewees, Cleveland)

25.11 Resolving differences in views about domestic violence and involving Women's Aid in a key position in multi-agency work are issues with which the projects in Sheffield, Greenwich, Derby and Cleveland have particularly attempted to grapple. Interviewees pointed out that the challenge and the group process involved could be beneficial processes in the evolution of group identity and cohesiveness, but that they could also result in inter-agency or inter-personal difficulties.

> "These issues are almost always painful and challenging for the

individuals involved on some level, and they bring up many issues of deeply held beliefs, and of agency loyalty and ethos, defensive feelings and personal experience (possibly experiences of abuse). Some forums prefer to avoid dealing with the issues and adopt a 'pretend' face of unity instead." (Interviewee, Sheffield)

25.12 The research interviews in a variety of study areas showed how easily misunderstandings could arise on a general level between participants, and, in this instance, concerning the involvement of refuge services specifically. Representatives of a variety of agencies might adopt a hectoring position, on occasion, or be too compliant. Others might feel belittled or misrepresented. Good communication skills, honesty, the building of trust, and the ability to admit mistakes and to learn from each other are qualities which all concerned may need to develop. Interviewees also pointed out, as noted in Section **5.12**, the need to sometimes "agree to disagree".

25.13 However, very real differences in politics, philosophy and attitude may exist between refuges which have their origins and roots in the social movement of women against domestic violence, and other agencies, particularly statutory ones, which do not share this history and politics. In a few localities surveyed during the mapping study, local refuges were very critical of their local inter-agency initiative and felt that it had nothing to do with them in any way. In others, the initiative had moved so far away from the ideals and practice of Women's Aid in its approaches and philosophy that it was almost as though it was a rival organisation, with little contact between the two. In one locality identified during the mapping study, the local refuge group had withdrawn from the inter-agency initiative as a protest against policies being adopted which, in their view,

ran counter to the interests of abused women and their children.

25.14 In some cases, Women's Aid and other refuges, which had been providing services, perhaps on a shoe-string, for many years, felt in the words of one refuge interviewee: "overtaken and wrong-footed by inter-agency work."

Refuge workers described how power differences could sometimes mean that they felt, or in reality were, intimidated by large statutory agencies, like the police, in terms of expressing their views, and that they also sometimes felt that their belief systems were incompatible with such agencies. **Many refuge workers who were interviewed welcomed inter-agency work in theory but felt that their work and their views were diluted beyond recognition, misunderstood, or not regarded as important by their local multi-agency initiative.**

25.15 The point was also strongly made that the involvement of Women's Aid could give credence to an inter-agency initiative, because, in the words of one agency interviewee: "they'd look pretty stupid if Women's Aid was not involved, wouldn't they?"

However, interviewees in the mapping study described how Women's Aid might then be placed in a position of appearing to sanction, by their membership of the group, policy or practice developments with which they disagreed but which they were powerless to influence. The multi-agency group could then use Women's Aid's membership as a selling point for the policy or practice development concerned. An awareness of pitfalls of this type could be of assistance in avoiding such outcomes.

25.16 In North Wales, on the other hand, Welsh Women's Aid was placed in a position, during the research period, of feeling that they needed to undertake a great deal of the work in order to keep the initiative afloat and to breathe life into it. **Thus, the situation in many localities,**

where Women's Aid was marginalised or isolated within the multi-agency initiative, contrasted with that in some others where Women's Aid did a great deal of the work and was faced with taking a leadership role with scant resources and facilities if the inter-agency initiative was to survive and flourish.

25.17 Overall, the evidence of the research supports the crucial importance of the role of Women's Aid and other refuges and women's organisations in multi-agency initiatives. The study evidence supports the need for all the agencies involved in inter-agency work, and the statutory agencies in particular, to take steps to ensure that Women's Aid and other refuge and advocacy services are not marginalised or isolated within the work, despite the difficulties described.

25.18 The research evidence also supports the need for, and desirability of, the Women's Aid federations, their members, and other refuge groups placing a greater priority on inter-agency work as a matter of principle, and developing, or continuing to develop, policy to inform their multi-agency practice. While all the federations have done some work on this area, WAFE already takes a particularly active role. However, the Women's Aid federations and other refuge providers may wish to take up the issue on a strategy-making level, producing recommendations or guidelines on refuge involvement in inter-agency forums.

25.19 Specialist support may need to be provided both for Women's Aid and for other refuge representatives in order to deal with issues such as those outlined above. Some multi-agency initiatives provide consultants or support/ supervision sessions for steering group or management members, for example, which can be particularly helpful to Women's Aid representatives. In addition, the Women's

Aid federations may be able to provide further support and guidance in the future and may wish to develop training initiatives on multi-agency work for refuge staff and for other agencies.

25.20 Where no refuges exist, difficulties may be experienced in setting up inter-agency initiatives and in maintaining the centrality of the perspective of abused women. As noted, domestic violence forums in such areas may have no representatives from the voluntary sector and few from front-line services. Guidance on what multi-agency tasks could be taken on in these circumstances and how to maintain a women-centred and effective approach to providing services for women is sometimes available from neighbouring forums or refuges or from the Women's Aid federations. Domestic violence forums are currently less common in rural areas, but may be expected to develop further in the future.

26. Equalities issues within multi-agency initiatives

26.1 Many inter-agency initiatives surveyed during the mapping study had not begun to take on issues of equality of opportunity on the grounds of race, religion, culture, sexuality, disability, age and social class. Black and disabled members of domestic violence forums expressed dissatisfaction at this situation to the research team in a variety of locations. Often, and especially where minority ethnic communities were relatively small, no members of minority groups or communities were involved with the multi-agency forum on any level, and members of some of these forums claimed that, as a result, they did not need to address the issue. Other interviewees, on the other hand, recognised that small communities may experience more isolation and the difficulties of women within them who

65

experienced domestic violence may be even more acute.

26.2 However, domestic violence forums investigated in various study areas were committed to integrating work on equal opportunities into the everyday practice of inter-agency work. In this commitment, these initiatives were more advanced than many other forums, and often enjoyed support from the equalities unit of their local authority where such a unit existed.

26.3 In the majority of the study areas, some work had commenced on issues of race and racism and on disability. Work on sexuality and class issues was much less well advanced. In some areas contacted during the mapping study, literature had been produced on the needs of lesbians experiencing domestic violence. Research projects on this issue were being conducted in a few metropolitan areas, for example. In the majority of cases, however, such work had been overlooked, and, in some initiatives, the subject had never been broached. Only a few forums showed any stated awareness of class issues. Issues about age were often overlooked but were taken up in Derby and Dorset, and the Walsall Domestic Violence Forum had set up an innovative Elderly Person's Task Group with a view to getting domestic violence in this context included within the local community care plan.

26.4 Work on anti-discriminatory practice which was taking place during the study included:

■ **making equal opportunities an integral part of all work undertaken, of all literature produced etc;**

■ **setting up specialist sub-groups** (eg, the Keighley Asian Women's Sub-group);

■ **aiming to achieve good representation of different groups within both the forum, and, importantly, its management;**

■ **producing specific literature and resource material** (eg, the Greenwich Domestic Violence Forum publication on domestic violence and Asian women);

■ **conducting research** (eg, research studies on the needs of black women, of disabled women, or of lesbians experiencing domestic violence);

■ **using good equal opportunities practice in selection and recruitment of employees;**

■ **translating material into a variety of locally-used languages and formats** (for example, on to audio-tape);

■ **providing interpreting services;**

■ **training;**

■ **using fully accessible venues as regards disability for all events and activities;**

■ **using fully accessible venues in other respects** (eg, avoiding locations in areas with known high levels of racism or homophobia which might not be comfortable for all members to attend);

■ **initiating new projects for specific groups of women and children** (eg, support groups for black women).

26.5 While agency workers interviewed in Derby, Sheffield and elsewhere pointed out that translation is only one small part of equalities practice, it is a key issue in raising awareness about domestic violence and providing services to abused women and children who do not speak or read English. Translation and interpretation are therefore regarded as important issues by many inter-agency projects. However, it was pointed out by a variety of interviewees that great care needs to be taken with translation and interpreting to ensure that they are culturally sensitive and aware of gender issues. In some of the study areas, all material was translated into community minority ethnic languages and into a variety of formats for the use of disabled women, and this work was routinely written into finding applications. For example, the Walsall Forum had produced leaflets in several languages which had been appreciated, according to interviewees.

An example of Good Practice

The Derby Domestic Violence Action Group routinely produces all material and publications in large print and on audio-tape, and provides translations into the major community languages. After some anxieties about the appropriateness and cultural sensitivity of translations, these are now routinely checked by a management committee member with the relevant expertise. All of this work is automatically, and without question, included in all budgeting, grant applications and other fund-raising. Resource shortage is a constant problem, however.

26.6 Representation issues in regard to equal opportunities and the issue of achieving a varied membership of the forum were a problem in most of the study areas. Despite some efforts to remedy under-representation, and while members of a variety of groups attend and express their views actively, the full domestic violence forums in Derby, Greenwich and Sheffield did not adequately reflect the rich social fabric, and the ethnic, class and cultural mix of the communities which they served during the study period. Few black organisations attended full forum meetings in these areas, for example. This was also the case for the forums in Cleveland, in Bristol (where, as noted, local forums serve particular areas of the city only), and in Walsall, all of which were situated in communities which were racially mixed to at least some degree. This lack of adequate representation, for example, from organisations of black women, was attributed by interviewees in various areas to the local inter-agency initiatives concerned being viewed as white organisations, and as unwelcoming. Few disabled members and organisations were involved in domestic violence forums in general (although in Derby, which has a particularly pro-active disability movement, disabled people and groups were more fully represented). A variety of interviewees suggested that instances of racist and other sorts of discriminatory practice, for example, ignoring disability or sexuality issues, could sometimes pass unchallenged in forum meetings as a result.

26.7 Conducting principled and extensive outreach work to minority groups or communities, supporting specific initiatives (eg, a funding application for a black women's refuge or support group), building a reputation for taking up equalities issues, and making meetings welcoming are just some examples of strategies which domestic violence forums have used to combat these difficulties.

26.8 In several areas studied, steering or management committees did not fully reflect the membership of their forum. As noted in previous sections, statutory agencies are frequently over-represented on management bodies for inter-agency initiatives. The research observations are that, very often, the same is true in respect to white non-disabled members. Forum members from other minority groups or organisations may also be under-represented on steering groups. In a few areas, deliberate attempts have been made to ensure that the steering or management committee contains members from a variety of racial, ethnic and cultural heritages and of different abilities, ages, class and professional backgrounds, and sexual orientation.

26.9 Good equal opportunities recruitment practice for employees was used in several of the main research areas during the study period. In others, recruitment and selection procedures could be improved, according to interviewees in those areas. Suggestions made to the researchers in this respect included using venues for interviews which are fully accessible to all, conducting employment outreach in minority communities, ensuring that selection panels are representative of a variety of groups, using good equal opportunities advertising and interviewing practice, and covering issues of anti-discriminatory practice in all interviews. Guidance on these issues is available from a variety of sources including WAFE, trade unions, some management advisory bodies and specialist organisations (eg, of disabled people).

26.10 Despite considerable progress in several of the study areas in taking on equal opportunities, the issues involved remain contentious, difficult and personally painful by their nature. In these areas, it has proved hard to keep equal opportunities issues on the agenda and has been a constant, and sometimes distressing, struggle for those involved. Interviewees in Derby, Cleveland, Sheffield, Greenwich and elsewhere suggested that domestic violence forums undertaking this work need to actively develop equalities practice within their management structures, within the forum as a whole, and within all work done, to avoid hurtful mistakes being made by members and to combat the frequently noted isolation of representatives from particular groups who may be unhappy with the potential burden of constantly having to be a spokesperson on the issue. Such a position, especially where the representative is unsupported by others within the group (where one disabled or black member participates in an otherwise white or non-disabled group, for example), may prove tiring, draining and distressing, according to interviewees themselves in this position. Some anxiety existed in some of the study areas that equalities practice would not go on developing if key individuals left or were absent.

26.11 Interviewees in almost all the areas surveyed emphasised that training is a major area of work in terms of equality. Even in multi-agency initiatives, where equalities practice is quite well developed, very little training is designed for specific groups of women (eg, women from minority ethnic communities or disabled women) as yet. Interviewees pointed out that training modules may not be sensitive to cultural, disability or sexuality issues, and that training needs to constantly change and evolve to take on diversity and anti-discriminatory practice in practical meaningful ways.

26.12 Current good practice is that all multi-agency training should include an addressing of issues of equal opportunities as an integral part of the programme offered. While attempts were made to honour this training commitment in at least three of the study areas, these attempts were not always successful and appeared from the research evidence to be a little ad hoc and piecemeal. Some initiatives provide equality training for management committee members and other forum members.

26.13 Despite the stated commitment of some multi-agency groups to integrating equalities work into all their projects, member agencies themselves sometimes overlook this work when representing or working alongside the inter-agency group.

26.14 The following suggestions were made during research interviews with regard to developing equalities practice:

■ **The adoption of full equal opportunities policies which are regularly reviewed and updated.**

■ The full involvement of a variety of organisations (eg, black or disabled women's groups) in both the forum and its management and the adoption of measures to combat the potential marginalisation of such groups.

■ The ongoing development of good equal opportunities employment practice (where relevant).

■ The establishment of an Equalities Sub-group of the domestic violence forum to take on particular pieces of work.

■ The possible setting-up of a general equalities advisory group or monitoring group to monitor and oversee all the inter-agency work undertaken. This group would be an advisory one and could therefore contain members who are not practising members of the forum. Thus, it would differ from the Equalities Sub-group of forum members suggested above.

■ The possible setting up of specialist advisory groups, for example, a black advisory or monitoring group, or a similar group of disabled women or of women with special needs. These groups would be charged with checking and monitoring all the activities of the inter-agency project in relation to equal opportunities and would be similar to the survivors advisory groups discussed in Section **27**.

■ The provision of equalities training for members of both steering groups or management committees and wider forums.

■ The integration of equalities issues into all multi-agency training offered and the inclusion of specialist training (eg, on the needs and rights of black women and children experiencing domestic violence).

■ The provision of consultants for representatives from minority communities who are black, disabled, lesbian etc as relevant in order to support particular members.

■ The provision of specialist support groups for members to turn to for help (eg, a disabled support group or a gay and lesbian support group).

■ The principled involvement of black women, disabled women, lesbians and other groups which may be discriminated against in positions of power within the organisation.

26.15 Setting up equality advisory groups (eg, a disabled advisory group), as noted above, to oversee and monitor work done is a practice which is beginning to be adopted by some domestic violence forums. The Cleveland Multi-agency Forum has conducted innovative work along these lines. However, some interviewees favoured the involvement of groups which may be discriminated against, in positions of power within the organisation, rather than in an advisory role as a matter of principle (although both might be possible). These interviewees often made the point that there can be a danger of 'hiving' off equalities work to a specialist group rather than maintaining it as an integral part of the project, and that forums which operate advisory groups need to be aware of this issue.

27. The involvement of women and children experiencing domestic violence in multi-agency initiatives

27.1 The involvement of abused women and children in multi-agency initiatives on domestic violence is a matter of current debate. Best practice in a wide range of caring services and research initiatives includes the involvement of 'user' groups, and informal accountability to them. In addition, Women's Aid and the refuge movement have always followed a policy of involving abused women and children in the provision of services. This appears to be rarely the case for domestic violence forums.

27.2 Various interviewees from a broad band of agencies and organisations made the point to the research team that it could be expected that women and children experiencing domestic violence might not know about inter-agency initiatives in their locality, but that they would, hopefully, benefit from improved agency coordination. The latter issue is discussed in the next section.

27.3 Women interviewed for the research study who were survivors of domestic violence were asked if they had heard of their local domestic violence forum and whether they were involved in it in any way. They were also asked whether they thought that women should be involved or consulted, and how this could be accomplished. Their views were solicited as to the type of work which they thought multi-agency initiatives should engage in.

27.4 Only 5 of the 70 women interviewed had heard of the multi-agency initiative in their area, and 8 thought that they might have heard of it but were not sure. Only two were involved in it on any level.

> "It sounds like a good idea but why don't women know about it? You say it's been going on for years but none of us have heard of it."
> (Woman interviewee, Cleveland)

Some women who have experienced domestic violence attend domestic violence forum meetings and make their views and experiences known. However, these members usually attend as representatives of professional organisations. In Walsall, women survivors attend forum meetings, although they are sometimes:

> " ... in awe of the conversations going on.... They need encour-

aging to speak and be more confident that they will be listened to and properly heard within the forum." (Agency interviewee, Walsall)

In one study area, the researchers were told that women referred to Victim Support by the police had heard of the domestic violence forum on occasion but that they tended to confuse it with the police domestic violence unit or think that they were the same thing. Other organisations which had contact with abused women and children in the study areas confirmed that the local inter-agency projects were rarely known or recognisable to the women who were referred to them.

27.5 Of the women interviewed, 60 out of the 70 felt that women's voices should be heard in their local domestic violence forum and that it was important that agencies listen to and learn from women who have experienced domestic violence. None felt that women should not be involved in the forum or that their views should not be represented, but 10 felt that they did not know enough about it or were not sure.

> "I think there should be regular representatives from the women. But you'd need to be sure they would be really listened to and people would take notice of what's said. If it doesn't get any further than that meeting it's pointless, it has to lead to a decision. Agencies need to take notice." (Woman interviewee, Walsall)

> "How do they know what to do if they don't ask the women in the situation? It doesn't make sense, does it?... It's stupid if they go and set up things without women knowing about it and without asking women what they need, doesn't make sense to me." (Woman interviewee, Cleveland)

"And it would be good if women had some say. If there was someone to tell about what happens, it would be helpful to the agencies. Also it would give women confidence because your confidence is knocked down by domestic violence – it would show women that there is a way out so that you know there is some escape.... If the agencies helped you together, women could go from strength to strength. Women can do it with some help." (Woman interviewee, Derby)

"It is totally ridiculous if the inter-agency projects don't listen to women and ask women what they need. How can they be sure they are doing the right thing if they don't consult women? How do they know? They have to ask. It's silly, stupid. Obviously they should be accountable to women and children." (Woman interviewee, Derby)

27.6 Of the interviewees who were not sure about how abused women could be involved, some felt that such involvement was not appropriate while the woman was in crisis.

"I think they need to know what it's like, but for us to tell them when we are sorted out. When we are all stressed out it doesn't come out clearly and they may think we are just hysterical! Later on we could explain better what it is really like." (Woman interviewee, Walsall)

"Well everyone is so different. I think women could only be like advisers, letting the experts know what it is like. I don't think they should have control of things. Which women would count most?" (Woman interviewee, Walsall)

27.7 A perhaps surprising research finding was that almost none of the women interviewed who were living in refuges which were actively participating in the local domestic violence forum knew about the forum in any of the study areas. Some inter-agency projects attempt to directly inform women who have experienced domestic violence about themselves through the active agency of Women's Aid and other refuges. While giving information to women and consulting them at refuge or house meetings or via other forums can be time-consuming, and many women may not be interested while negotiating the life crisis of living in a refuge, refuges are, in fact, in a key position to pass on information and ideas. Even though refuge workers are often over-loaded, as discussed above, it has been suggested that, where an inter-agency domestic violence forum exists, refuges could take on this role in an active, principled and consistent way, as an accepted part of their work.

"If the staff hold a residents meeting to inform us about the services and what is available. Refuges could do more of that – to inform women." (Woman interviewee, Derby)

"It would be good to let women know about it – tell them when they come into the refuge and explain what it is and give you a leaflet to read about it – then you could get involved if you wanted." (Woman interviewee, Derby)

27.8 Some of the specific suggestions made to the research team by women interviewees for how abused women and children could be involved in inter-agency domestic violence work and how their views could be considered are as follows:

■ Listening to women.

" ... agencies have got to *really* understand. They should listen to women and to what women who have suffered violence have to say." (Woman interviewee, Derby)

" .... they should listen to women – and especially to disabled women. Should it be accountable? Yes of course, but that's not the sort of thing they do." (Woman interviewee, Derby)

■ **Women to fill out a questionnaire** (eg, while resident in a refuge) on their wants and needs and on what the inter-agency initiative could do.

■ **Refuges to take a much more active role** in terms of feeding information about the domestic violence forum to women at refuge meetings and feeding ideas from women back to the forum (as noted above). While many women would not be interested in this information, some would. Clearly, the women interviewed in the study felt that they would like to have known about and to have had the chance to have been involved, even if they declined it.

■ **Snappy slogans and campaigns on television** and in the cinema, on local radio etc.

■ **More publicity and awareness-raising** directed towards women experiencing domestic violence about the inter-agency project and about the fact that refuges and other services now exist.

"The whole world needs to know – so women will no longer put up with it. Everyone needs to know about it. To break the silence." (Woman interviewee, Derby)

" ... more publicity would be good. To say that women don't have to suffer the violence and there *is* somewhere to go. We need: publicity; raising awareness; letting women know refuges and hostels

exist." (Woman interviewee, Derby)

■ **Abused women to have more opportunities to speak about their experiences** at worker training sessions and to have formal and recognised input into training programmes.

■ **Further participation of domestic violence survivors** in new projects for abused women and children set up by the domestic violence forum.

■ **The setting up of a local domestic violence 'ombudsman' post** in the community.

27.9 In any development involving abused women, both agency and women interviewees made it clear that it is important that women are "not used, exploited and then not compensated in any way" (Agency interviewee, Sheffield). There are many ways that these issues can be addressed, including payment for work done, payment of transport costs and other expenses incurred, crèche provision for meetings, etc.

27.10 One of the practice developments which is currently being debated and tried out within domestic violence forums and other inter-agency initiatives is the establishing of advisory or monitoring groups for survivors of domestic violence. Such groups are able to monitor and to have input into all policy and practice work conducted by the initiative. The Cleveland Multi-agency Forum has set up a survivors group of this nature and other forums are considering doing so.

27.11 Due to the newness of this work, contentious issues and disagreements are bound to arise and should be expected as part of the process. In a few areas, there has been some debate as to whether such a group could also be a self-help group. While this could hopefully be the case in practice, research respondents pointed out that the monitoring and advisory work of a survivors advisory group is something rather different and is, as yet, unfamiliar to most domestic violence forums. The potential of this practice initiative was viewed with enthusiasm by interviewees in the areas where it was developing.

27.12 While there are very clear issues of equal opportunities and of accountability in the setting up of a rather random and ad hoc survivors group in a monitoring capacity, *informal* monitoring of this type is a potential way forward. The research indicates that it would be a worthwhile endeavour for domestic violence forums to continue to attempt to evolve in this difficult but innovative direction. There is no easy answer to this issue, and no one is sure, at the point of writing, quite how to proceed. This does not mean, however, that the attempt should be abandoned. It is worth noting that some of the American domestic abuse intervention projects maintain that accountability to groups of abused women is of crucial importance to the development of the work.

27.13 Thus, two of the major suggestions arising from the report on the involvement of women and children who are experiencing domestic violence are:

a) **the active involvement of Women's Aid and refuges in facilitating such involvement;**

b) **the possible setting up of survivors advisory or monitoring groups.**

Further guidance from the Women's Aid federations would be of assistance on these issues.

28. Inter-agency coordination and customer satisfaction

Women's views of services received

28.1 Women interviewed for the study were asked about how well coordinated services and agencies in their area were, and about the specific service which they and their children, where relevant, had received. Interviewees were also questioned about each of the different agencies which they had approached for assistance, about the details of each experience, and about their view of service provision and delivery, in addition to co-ordination of services. However, in-depth questioning was not pursued in the interviews in relation to the fine details and complexities of services received.

28.2 The majority of women interviewed felt that the agencies which they had approached for help had co-ordinated their services fairly successfully. More of the interviewees were satisfied in this respect in Derby than in Cleveland and Walsall, although the differences were very small between Derby and Cleveland.

28.3 The numbers of women satisfied with the services they received varied for the different agencies in each locality and were generally very mixed. **Where police domestic violence units existed, interviewees often singled these out for praise, in comparison with other police services. The great majority of women interviewed were extremely satisfied with the services received from refuges in all the areas.** Overall, refuges elicited by far the most satisfaction from women, as compared with other agencies.

28.4 During the mapping study, some inter-agency forum coordinators and refuge workers expressed anxiety that multi-agency coordination could lead to increased 'surveillance' of abused women and children. For one woman interviewed for the study, this had indeed been the case and agencies had liaised extensively without informing her, leading to stated concerns by herself and by some involved agencies about the possibly intrusive nature and the extent of the inter-agency cooperation which had occurred. The possibility of multi-agency work in general moving in this direction in terms of social control and civil liberties issues was touched on briefly in Chapter 2. Multi-agency domestic violence initiatives, in contrast to the situation for child protection, are not generally concerned with specific cases, and a 'case conference' model of work is not appropriate. However, domestic violence forums may need to exercise caution and vigilance in ensuring that inappropriate networking and breaches of confidentiality do not take place in relation to individuals.

Improvements in women's and children's safety and in services provided

28.5 In answer to research questions about whether the local inter-agency project had improved women and children's safety or the provision and delivery of services (rather, perhaps, than being a 'talking shop'), a very large number of respondents from agencies were not sure. Many made such statements as: "it must have". The research study was unable to monitor these supposed improvements directly and very few inter-agency forums have engaged in evaluation exercises themselves. In any case, the effects of improved coordination are hard to gauge. **However, there was some tentative general evidence from the research interviews that the services which women and children receive had been improved by some of the new projects established by forums (eg, information lines), by the implementation of practice guidelines by agencies, and by the provision of domestic violence training. The preventative and educational work which inter-agency projects initiate (eg, in schools) has a different long-term goal and cannot be measured by any conventional means.**

28.6 In the three main study areas, some agency interviewees described improvements in service provision which they related to the inter-agency initiative. As an example, in a Walsall agency interviewees noted improvements in local knowledge about domestic violence and where to turn for help, in the use of security alarms, in the arrangements for women to make benefit claims in a safe way, and in the use of confidentiality. All of these improvements were attributed to the work of the local forum.

Summary

■ While the voluntary sector is represented in most inter-agency domestic violence forums, in some it is not. The study interviews provided evidence, however, that the participation of voluntary sector agencies is vital in achieving inter-agency coordination.

■ Even where there is some involvement, the voluntary sector in general appears to be frequently under-represented on multi-agency forums, and on their steering groups or management bodies in particular, so that membership may appear skewed towards the statutory sector. It was also the case during the study that power differences between statutory and voluntary agencies played a role in deterring some voluntary organisations from taking part. However, voluntary sector agencies need to make a stated commitment to the work, to 'sign up to it'.

■ While Women's Aid is accepted as the lead specialist agency in dealing with domestic violence, the Women's Aid federations and refuge groups are, in fact, small organisations, often under-funded, with little realistic power. It can be difficult in inter-agency projects to attempt to equalise power differences between member agencies and to maintain the key role of the refuge movement as objectively more powerful agencies, such as the police and the local authority, become involved. There can be a tendency for the statutory agencies to 'take over' inter-agency work, and for Women's Aid and other refuges to be marginalised in consequence. In some areas, it was clear that refuges were regarded as just one voluntary agency among many, instead of as the leading specialist organisation in service provision.

■   However, the full involvement of refuges is not always possible due to their continual crisis work and, frequently, their low staffing ratios. It can also be an isolating experience when only one or two representatives from refuges are involved in an inter-agency initiative, and have to push continually for their views and the views of abused women to be taken seriously.

■   Strategies to deal with these difficulties include refuges taking a major role within the multi-agency initiative as an agreed principle of its operation. In some areas, Women's Aid formally takes the chair of the organisation, or occupies a reserved place on the steering group. In others, Women's Aid is far from marginalised and may take a leadership role, often with scant resources.

■   However, very real differences in politics and philosophy may exist between refuges which have their origins and roots in the social movement of women against domestic violence, and other agencies, particularly statutory ones, which do not share this history and politics.

■   The study evidence supports the need for all the agencies involved in inter-agency work, and the statutory agencies in particular, to take concrete steps to ensure that Women's Aid and other refuges maintain a central position within the work.

■   There is a need for the Women's Aid federations, their member refuges and other refuge groups to place a greater priority on inter-agency work and to further develop policy to inform their multi-agency practice. The federations and other refuge providers may wish to take up this issue on a strategy-making level, producing recommendations or guidelines on refuge involvement in inter-agency forums.

■   Where no refuges exist, difficulties may be experienced in setting up inter-agency initiatives and in maintaining the centrality of the perspective of abused women, although guidance on these issues can be sought from neighbouring forums or refuges, from consultants or trainers, from well-established forums or from the Women's Aid federations.

■   Many inter-agency initiatives surveyed during the mapping study had not begun to take on issues of equality of opportunity on the grounds of race, religion, culture, sexuality, disability, age and social class. However, some domestic violence forums were committed to integrating work on equal opportunities into the everyday practice of inter-agency work.

■   Only 5 of the 70 women interviewed had heard of the multi-agency initiative in their area. Only two were involved in it on any level. Sixty out of the 70 felt that women's voices should be heard in their local domestic violence forum and that it was important that agencies listen to and learn from women who have experienced domestic violence. Surprisingly, almost none of the women interviewed who were living in refuges which were actively participating in the local domestic violence forum knew about the forum in any of the study areas. Refuges are, in fact, in a key position to pass on information and ideas. Refuges could take on this role in an active, principled and consistent way.

■   An innovative new development is the setting up of survivors advisory groups to informally oversee and monitor the work of the local forum.

■ The majority of the women interviewed felt that the agencies which they had approached for help had coordinated their services fairly successfully. Degrees of satisfaction with services received from individual agencies were very mixed, however. Where police domestic violence units existed, interviewees were often more satisfied with their services than with other police services. The great majority of women interviewed were extremely satisfied with the services received from refuges.

■ There was some anxiety that multi-agency coordination could lead to increased 'surveillance' of abused women and children. While individual case work by inter-agency forums is uncommon, caution and vigilance may need to be exercised to ensure that inappropriate networking or breaches of confidentiality do not take place.

■ While there was some evidence that the safety of women and children had been directly improved by multi-agency coordination and by the provision of services by inter-agency forums, doubts about these issues were expressed and no firm conclusion could be drawn.

Part III

Conclusions and suggestions for future developments

Chapter 10

Conclusions and key issues

29. Assessing the effectiveness of multi-agency forums

29.1 While innovative coordinating, preventative and educational work had been undertaken in many areas investigated during the study, in others very little had been done and there were suggestions that multi-agency initiatives could use up resources and energy, do little, waste time, and divert funds and attention away from the provision of refuges and emergency services.

29.2 Many interviewees pointed out that the 'bottom line', as regards accountability and effectiveness, should be whether the activities of a domestic violence inter-agency initiative have an effect on improving the safety of abused women and children (see also Section **6.16** and Section **28**). Although the issues in question are extremely complex, some of the factors which appeared during the study to lead to effective, rather than ineffective, action are:

■ Active involvement of statutory agencies, at both policy-making and practitioner level, with senior management support. These agencies to include the police; local authority special units, housing, social services and education departments; probation; legal and court personnel; and health services.

■ The full participation of Women's Aid and local refuge services, and the use of concrete strategies, not only to avoid their marginalisation, but also to actively promote their central involvement.

■ Active participation of community, grass-roots and women's organisations.

■ Active involvement of Victim Support, and of all relevant voluntary sector agencies both at practitioner and at management level (locally and nationally).

■ Consistent, committed, active attendance and membership, with members attending as agreed representatives of their agencies where possible.

■ The adoption of *guiding principles* and the development of common agreements about domestic violence.

■ Clear and well developed *aims and objectives, equal opportunities policies* and other *terms of reference*, regularly reviewed.

■ A workable structure enabling clarity and lines of accountability, but avoiding layers of bureaucracy, perhaps involving an active and representative steering committee and sub-groups.

■ The availability of at least some resources for activities, projects taken on and coordination work, and for servicing the forum.

■ If possible, the employment of a co-ordinator or development worker with administrative support.

■ The relating of all activities to meeting the needs, and increasing the safety, of abused women and children and to decreasing domestic violence.

■ The development of concrete initiatives and activities which are within the capabilities of the forum.

■ The integration of equalities issues into all work done.

■ The involvement of, and some form of informal accountability to, women survivors of domestic violence and their children.

■ The use of evaluation and monitoring processes in specific relation to work done and its effectiveness.

30. Pioneering development or smoke-screen?

30.1 Various interviewees suggested that inter-agency coordination could be largely ineffective or could act as a "way of saving face and looking as though you are doing something" (Agency interviewee), unless it was positioned within a supportive policy and practice framework at both local and central government level.

> "The forums can just be for talking and they achieve or do nothing – can become a waste of people's time. It can be a smoke-screen, it can remove the politics. But having a coordinator really helps. And they need policy decisions and support both from local government but also from central government – if the idea is going to grow and develop. The Home Office Circular is not enough."

> "You have to have strategic development. Have to look across the board, not just at your own agency. Everyone tends to think its someone else's responsibility which leads to things not being done. Getting motivation is sometimes difficult. It needs to be

in a wider policy context of commitment and resources." (Agency interviewees, two different areas)

30.2 While many interviewees were enthusiastic about the potential of inter-agency work as the 'next stage' of combating domestic violence after the provision of basic services, respondents in a considerable number of areas and agencies pointed out that increased coordination is of little use if the resources and services needed are not in place.

30.5 Ellen Pence, the former co-ordinator of the Duluth Domestic Abuse Intervention Project, has stated in several national training seminars run in this country for inter-agency workers and others under the auspices of the London Borough of Hammersmith and Fulham that: **it is pointless to improve coordination if the system being coordinated is inadequate or inappropriate.** Some of the study interviewees from women's organisations and from the refuge network independently corroborated this view and suggested that inter-agency work can act as a smoke-screen or as a talking shop which disguises inaction and poor services. These wider issues about inter-agency work, resources and effectiveness in the context of government support and political developments are discussed further, in the following concluding section.

31. Inter-agency work in the wider national context

31.1 It is clear from the Inter-agency Circular, *Inter-agency coordination to tackle domestic violence* (Home Office, 1995) that responsibility for the success of multi-agency approaches to domestic violence does not lie with local agencies alone. In Section **4**, outlining the government's approach to inter-agency work (Home Office, 1995, p 9, S4), the Circular states that the Home Office has the lead responsibility to coordinate the response of central government to domestic violence, chairing the Official and Ministerial Inter-departmental Groups on domestic violence. The Lord Chancellor's Department, the Law Officer's Department, the CPS, the Departments of Environment, Health, Social Security, the Department for Education and Employment, the Welsh, Scottish and Northern Ireland Offices and the Treasury all participate in these groups (Home Office, 1995, p 9, S4.1). In addition, although the approach of the government is said to be "based on the premise that domestic violence is a serious crime which must not be tolerated" (Home Office, 1995, p 9, S4.2) with a priority given to stopping the violence occurring, the Circular also speaks of a need for the commitment and involvement of local agencies working together to provide help and support to those experiencing domestic violence and to develop preventive strategies.

31.2   The Circular lists a range of actions which assume the participation of a very wide range of statutory and voluntary agencies, and would involve these agencies having both the necessary resources and, in some cases, the necessary mandate and powers under the law to carry them out. The list of action points comprises the following (Home Office, 1995, p 9, S4.3):

■   Encouraging those who are experiencing domestic violence to come forward and address their situation through the help that is available.

■   Addressing the needs of children affected by domestic violence.

■   The provision of safe accommodation and support services, both emergency and long term, for women and their children who feel compelled to leave the family home.

■   Ensuring adequate legal protection under the civil and criminal law.

■   Bringing perpetrators to justice.

■   Assisting perpetrators to understand and address the reasons for and consequences of their offending behaviour in order to stop the abuse.

■   Prevention through education and community initiatives including those that challenge beliefs that condone and reproduce violent behaviour in intimate relationships.

31.3   However, none of the agency representatives interviewed in the course of the research had knowledge of further specific guidance from ministries other than the Home Office on the need to work within a coordinated multi-agency strategy on domestic violence issues or on how to do so. The only guidance mentioned of this kind was that issued by ACOP (1996). As noted, there has also been a recently published report of two conferences held in March 1995 by the Social Services Inspectorate of the DoH (Ball, 1996). This very useful publication contains much valuable information from the conferences and makes suggestions as to the relevance of the inter-agency approach to domestic violence for social services and its importance for their work.

31.4   Similar initiatives from other ministries and from the health division of the DoH would be very welcome. However, although such awareness-raising events are very valuable, they are not, in themselves, sufficient to ensure the involvement of representatives from the full range of agencies whose work has a potential to provide the kind of co-ordinated action that is necessary. As discussed in Part II, even in relatively well established multi-agency initiatives, there is very patchy participation by some statutory agencies, such as some relevant local authority departments and the various branches of the health services, and by areas of the criminal justice system, especially those other than the police and the probation service.

31.5   As a number of the agency representatives pointed out, and as noted in

Sections **17-21**, the lack of specific guidance on inter-agency working from relevant ministries can often be expected to lead to low priority being given to work on domestic violence either within individual agencies or in relation to inter-agency work. For example, a representative of a community health trust in one of the study areas, when asked whether she could continue her present level of commitment to the forum, said that it would depend on the way in which priorities were set. In her opinion, echoed by others, it would only be if such work was designated at national level by the relevant ministry as part of the core job of agency workers that participation could be ensured and protected, and the work be given a sufficient degree of importance within the agency concerned.

31.6 Other agency interviewees were of a similar opinion and a number also referred to a combination of financial and statutory limitations on the ability of agencies to provide effective support for the aims enunciated in the Inter-agency Circular, as quoted above. Such views suggest, perhaps, a need for the Inter-departmental Groups, especially at ministerial level, to discuss the content of proposed legislation from the viewpoint of its impact on the provision of effective services for safety as well as the prevention of domestic violence.

31.7 As previously discussed, many interviewees were concerned at the lack of secure funding, and of a national funding strategy for refuges, and the possible effect this created of inter-agency services competing with refuge-based advocacy and support services for scarce resources. Such problems were viewed as a severe drawback to the almost entirely local and piecemeal nature of funding for multi-agency initiatives, the majority of which have no resources at all. This was sometimes seen as a matter of central government willing the ends, but not providing the means, to carry out effective

inter-agency work at a time of retrenchment of expenditure.

31.8 Thus, two of the major conclusions of this study are that further national and local guidance, and adequate resourcing for inter-agency domestic violence work are essential if the approach is to be successful.

31.9 In summing up, although much good work is being carried out, local multi-agency initiatives can only develop as a national coordinated response to domestic violence within a context of clear understandings about the minimal level of necessary resource provision, so that the co-ordination of services is not being carried out at the expense of resources for basic refuge, advocacy and support services. At local level in the statutory services, there is a need for commitment at a senior rank to policy initiatives on domestic violence which are carried through into practice within and between agencies as part of an overall strategy. However, these developments need to be informed by grass-roots practitioner knowledge and by the experience of refuges, independent women's advocacy services, and the Women's Aid federations.

31.10 In order for such multi-agency work to be seen as a core part of the function of statutory agencies at local level, all government departments participating in the Inter-departmental Groups need to issue guidance to relevant agencies at the appropriate level directly, not only to indicate the seriousness of the effects of domestic violence for the health and well-being of large numbers of women and children, but also to encourage their active participation in multi-agency work and to indicate how such work is to be resourced.

31.11 For the effective and consistent participation of the necessary range of agencies, work on domestic violence issues needs to be a designated part of the job descriptions of representatives of statutory agencies. Officers could also be officially released from other duties in order to participate in multi-agency initiatives as an agreed part of their workload.

31.12 Such measures would enable the innovative work already done to be carried forward free of the suspicion that it may be in part a cheap option and a face saver in lieu of a comprehensive national policy.

31.13 There may also be a need for communication nationally between the wide variety of multi-agency forums now being established, possibly through the setting up of a national network or newsletter, or some other similar development. Further training initiatives on how to conduct inter-agency work on domestic violence would also be of benefit.

31.14 Further, as noted in Section **25**, it would be of great benefit if the Women's Aid federations were to further develop national strategies, guidelines, and training in relation to the participation of refuges in inter-agency work.

31.15 The research clearly showed the amount of energy and imagination already going into the development of inter-agency work, and its potential to develop further as a creative, exciting way forward. Inter-agency initiatives could, in the future, be of major importance in building awareness about domestic violence and its consequences, in creating and coordinating effective and wide-reaching services and hopefully in helping to create a society which no longer condones such violence or minimises its impact.

References

Adams, D. (1988) 'Treatment models of men who batter: a pro-feminist analysis', in K. Yllo and M. Bograd (eds), *Feminist perspectives on wife abuse*, London: Sage, pp 176-99.

Arblaster, L., Conway, J., Foreman, A. and Hawtin, M. (1996), *Asking the impossible? Inter-agency working to address the housing, health and social care needs of people in ordinary housing*, Bristol: The Policy Press.

Association of Chief Officers of Probation (1992; revised 1996), *Position statement on domestic violence*, London: ACOP.

Ball, M. (1996) *Domestic violence and social care: a report on two conferences held by the Social Services Inspectorate*, Social Services Inspectorate, DoH.

Barron, J. (1990) *Not worth the paper?: the effectiveness of legal protection for women and children experiencing domestic violence*, WAFE.

Barron, J., Harwin, N. and Singh, T. (1992) *Women's Aid Federation (England): written evidence to the House of Commons Home Affairs Committee Inquiry into Domestic Violence*, WAFE.

Binney, V. (1981) 'Domestic violence: battered women in Britain in the seventies', in Cambridge Women's Studies Group (eds), *Women in society*, London: Virago, pp 115-26.

Binney, V., Harkell, G. and Nixon, J. (1981) *Leaving violent men: a study of refuges and housing for battered women*, WAFE.

Binney, V., Harkell, G. and Nixon, J. (1985) 'Refuges and housing for battered women', in J. Pahl (ed), *Private violence and public policy*, London: Routledge and Kegan Paul, pp 166-78.

Blagg, H,. Pearson, G., Smith, D. and Stubbs, P. (1988) 'Inter-agency co-operation: rhetoric and reality', in T. Hope and M. Shaw (eds), *Communities and crime reduction*, London: HMSO.

Cahn, N. and Lerman, L. (1991) 'Prosecuting woman abuse', in M. Steinman (ed), *Woman battering: policy responses*, Cincinnati, Ohio: Anderson Publishing.

Convention of Scottish Local Authorities (1991) *Women and violence*, Convention of Scottish Local Authorities.

Cretney, A. and Davis, G. (1996) 'Prosecuting domestic assault', *Criminal Law Review*, March, pp 162-74.

Department of Health (1988) *Working together: a guide to arrangements for inter-agency cooperation for the protection of children from abusers*, DoH.

Department of Health (1994; 1995) *Tackling drugs together*, DoH Green Paper and White Paper.

Dobash, R.E. and Dobash, R.P. (1980) *Violence against wives*, London: Open Books.

Dobash, R.E. and Dobash, R.P. (1988) 'Research as social action: the struggle for battered women', in K. Yllo and M. Bograd (eds), *Feminist perspectives on wife abuse*, London: Sage, pp 51-74.

Dominy, N. and Radford, L. (1996) *Domestic violence in Surrey: developing an effective inter-Agency response*, Surrey County Council and Roehampton Institute.

Dublin Women's Aid (1995) *Discussion document on an inter-agency approach to domestic violence*, Dublin Women's Aid.

Dunhill, C. (ed) (1989) *The boys in blue: women's challenge to the police*, London: Virago.

Edelson, J. (1991) 'Coordinated community responses', in M. Steinman (ed), *Woman battering: policy responses*, Cincinnati, Ohio: Anderson Publishing.

Edwards, S. (1986) 'The real risks of violence behind doors', *New Law Journal*, 136/628, pp 1191-93.

Edwards, S. (1989) *Policing domestic violence*, London: Sage.

Farmer, E. and Owen, M. (1993) *Decision-making, intervention and outcome in child protection work*, London: DoH.

Gardiner, J. (forthcoming) 'The more things change, the more they stay the same', in N. Harwin, E. Malos and G. Hague (eds), *Inter-agency responses and domestic violence*, London: Whiting and Birch.

Gelsthorpe, L. (1985) *The community service volunteers/Kent Initiative*, Report IV, Community Service Volunteers.

Gill, K. and Pickles, T. (eds) (1989) *Active collaboration: joint practice and youth strategies*, ITRC.

Goolkasian, G. (1986) *Confronting domestic violence: a guide for criminal justice agencies*, Washington DC, US Department of Justice, National Institute of Justice.

Goss, S. and Kent, C. (1995) *Health and housing: working together? A review of the extent of inter-agency working*, Bristol: The Policy Press.

Government reply to the Third Report from the Home Affairs Committee (1993) Session 1992-93, HC245, London: HMSO.

Grace, S. (1995) *Policing domestic violence in the 1990s*, Home Office Research Study 139, HMSO.

Hague, G. and Malos, E. (1993) *Domestic violence: action for change*, Cheltenham: New Clarion Press.

Hague, G., Malos, E. and Dear, W. (1995a) *Against domestic violence: inter-agency initiatives* (SAUS Working Paper 127), Bristol: The Policy Press.

Hague, G., Malos, E. and Dear, W. (1995b), 'Inter-agency approaches to domestic violence', *Probation Journal*, vol 42, no 4, pp 220-25.

Hague, G., Kelly, L., Malos, E. and Mullender, A. (1996), *Children, domestic violence and refuges: a study of needs and responses*, WAFE.

Hallet, C. (1995) *Inter-agency coordination in child protection*, London: HMSO.

Hanmer, J., and Saunders, S. (1984) *Well-founded fear: a community study of violence to women*, London: Hutchinson.

Harwin, N., Malos, E. and Hague, G. (eds) (forthcoming) *Inter-agency responses and domestic violence*, London: Whiting and Birch.

Hester, M. and Radford, J. (1996) *Domestic violence and child contact arrangements in England and Denmark*, Bristol: The Policy Press.

Holder, R. (forthcoming) 'Creating an unholy alliance', in N. Harwin, E. Malos and G. Hague (eds), *Inter-agency responses and domestic violence*, London: Whiting and Birch.

Home Affairs Committee (1993) *Inquiry into domestic violence*, London: HMSO

Home Office (1986) Circular 69/86, *Violence against women*, London: Home Office.

Home Office (1990) Circular 60/90, *Domestic violence*, London: Home Office.

Home Office (1991) *Safer communities: the local delivery of crime prevention through the partnership approach*, London: Home Office.

Home Office (1995) *Inter-agency circular: inter-agency co-ordination to tackle domestic violence*, Home Office and Welsh Office.

Home Office Crime Prevention Unit (1987) *The Five Towns Initiative*.

Howard, R., Beadle, P. and Maitland, J. (1993) *Across the divide: building community partnerships to tackle drug misuse*, DoH.

Hudson, B. (1987) 'Collaboration in social welfare: a framework for analysis', *Policy and Politics*, vol 15, no 4, pp 175-89.

Kitzinger, J. and Hunt, K. (1993) *Evaluation of Edinburgh District Council's Zero Tolerance campaign*, Edinburgh District Council Women's Committee.

Law Commission (1992) *Family law: domestic violence and occupation of the family home*, Report No 207, London: HMSO.

Leeds Inter-Agency Project (1993) *Violence against women by known men: training pack*, Leeds Inter-Agency Project,

Sahara Black Women's Refuge and Leeds Women's Aid.

Liddle, A. and Bottoms, A. (1994) *The Five Towns Initiative: key findings and implications from a retrospective research analysis*, Home Office.

Liddle, M. and Gelsthorpe, L. (1994a) *Inter-agency crime prevention: organising local delivery*, Police Research Group Crime Prevention Unit Series, Paper 52, Home Office.

Liddle, M. and Gelsthorpe, L. (1994b) *Crime prevention and inter-agency co-operation*, Police Research Group Crime Prevention Unit Series, Paper 53, Home Office.

Liddle, M. and Gelsthorpe, L. (1994c) *Inter-agency crime prevention: further issues*, Police Research Group Crime Prevention Unit Series, Supplementary Paper to Papers 52 and 53, Home Office.

Lloyd, C. (1994) *The welfare net: how well does the net work?*, Oxford: Oxford Brookes University.

London Borough of Greenwich (1995) *Asian women and domestic violence: information for advisers*, London Borough of Greenwich, Greenwich Asian Women's Centre, Greenwich Asian Women's Project.

London Borough of Hammersmith and Fulham Community Safety Unit (1991) *Challenging domestic violence: a training and resource pack*, London Borough of Hammersmith and Fulham.

London Borough of Islington (1992) *A good practice guide: working with those who have experienced domestic violence*, London Borough of Islington.

London Borough of Islington (1995a) *The needs and experiences of black and minority ethnic women experiencing domestic violence*, London Borough of Islington.

London Borough of Islington (1995b) *Stop: striving to prevent domestic violence; an activity pack for working with children and young people*, London Borough of Islington.

McGregor, H. and Hopkins, A. (1991) *Working for change: the movement against domestic violence*, London: Allen and Unwin.

McMahon, M. and Pence, E. (forthcoming) 'Legal advocacy; audits and activities', in N. Harwin, E. Malos and G. Hague (eds), *Inter-agency responses and domestic violence*, London: Whiting and Birch.

Malos, E. (1993) *You've got no life: homelessness and the use of bed and breakfast hotels*, University of Bristol. School of Applied Social Studies.

Malos, E. and Hague, G. (1993) *Domestic violence and housing: local authority responses to women and children escaping violence in the home*, WAFE and University of Bristol.

Mama, A. (1989) *The hidden struggle: statutory and voluntary responses to violence against black women in the home*, London, London Race and Housing Research Unit.

Maynard, M. (1985) 'The response of social workers to domestic violence', in J. Pahl (ed) *Private violence and public policy*, London: Routledge and Kegan Paul, pp 125-41.

Moelwyn-Hughes, A. (forthcoming) 'Sharing the responsibility: reaching joint agreements on domestic violence policy', in N. Harwin, E. Malos and G. Hague (eds), *Inter-agency responses and domestic violence*, London: Whiting and Birch.

Morley, R. and Mullender, A. (1994) *Preventing domestic violence to women*, Home Office Police Research Group Crime Prevention Series Paper 49, Home Office.

Mullender, A. (forthcoming) 'Social service responses to domestic violence: the inter-agency challenge', in N. Harwin, E. Malos and G. Hague (eds), *Inter-agency responses and domestic violence*, London: Whiting and Birch.

Mullender, A. and Morley, R. (eds) (1994) *Children living with domestic violence*, Whiting and Birch.

National Association of Local Government Women's Committees (now Women in Local Authority Network) (1989; currently being updated) *Responding with authority: local authority initiatives to counter violence against women*, NALGWC.

National Children Homes (1994) *The hidden victims*, NCH Action for Children.

National Inter-Agency Working Party Report (1992) *Domestic violence*, Victim Support.

Pahl, J. (ed) (1985) *Private violence and public policy: the needs of battered women and the response of the public service*, London: Routledge and Kegan Paul.

Parliamentary Select Committee on Violence in Marriage (1975) *Report from the Select Committee on violence in marriage*, London: HMSO.

Patel, P. (forthcoming) 'The multi-agency approach to domestic violence: a panacea or obstacle to women's struggles for freedom from violence?', in N. Harwin, E. Malos and G. Hague (eds), *Inter-agency responses and domestic violence*.

Pence, E. (1988) *Batterers' programs: shifting from community collusion to community confrontation*, Domestic Abuse Intervention Project, Duluth.

Pence, E. and Shepard, M. (1988) 'Integrating feminist theory and practice: the challenge of the battered women's movement', in K. Yllo and M. Bograd (eds), *Feminist perspectives on wife abuse*, London: Sage, pp 282-98.

Pizzey, E. (1974) *Scream quietly or the neighbours will hear*, Harmondsworth: Penguin.

Rose, H. (1985) 'Women's refuges: creating new forms of welfare?', in C. Ungerson (ed), *Women and social policy*, London: Macmillan, pp 243-59.

Russell, M. (1989) *Taking stock: survey into refuge provision in London*, Southwark Borough Council.

Sampson, A. (1991) *Lessons from a Victim Support Crime Prevention Project*, Home Office Crime Prevention Unit, Paper 25, Home Office.

Sampson, A., Smith, D., Pearson, G., Blagg, H. and Stubbs, P. (1991) 'Gender issues in inter-agency relations: police, probation and social services', in P. Abbott and C. Wallace (eds), *Gender, power and sexuality*, London: Macmillan.

Sampson, A., Stubbs, P., Smith, D., Pearson, G. and Blagg. H. (1988) 'Crime, localities and the multi-agency approach', *British Journal of Criminology*, vol 28, pp 478-93.

Smith, G. and Cantley, C. (1985) *Assessing health care: a study in organizational evaluation*, Oxford: Oxford University Press.

Smith, L. (1989) *Domestic violence: an overview of the literature*, Home Office Research Studies, No 107, London: HMSO.

Smith, R., Gaster, L., Harrison, L., Martin, L., Means, R. and Thistlethwaite, P. (1993) *Working together for better community care*, Bristol: SAUS Publications.

Southall Black Sisters (1989) 'Two struggles: challenging male violence and the police', in C. Dunhill, *The boys in blue: women's challenge to the police*, London: Virago, pp 38-44.

United Nations (1986) *Report of the Expert Group Meeting on Violence in the Family*, United Nations.

United Nations (1990) *Convention on the Elimination of all Forms of Discrimination Against Women*, United Nations.

United Nations (1993) *Declaration on the Elimination of Violence Against Women*, United Nations.

Walker, J. and McNicol, L. (1994) *Policing domestic violence: protection, prevention or prudence*, Newcastle, Relate Centre for Family Studies.

Webb, A. (1991) 'Coordination, a problem in public sector management', *Policy and Politics*, vol 19, no 4, pp 229-42.

Women's National Commission (1985) *Violence against women: report of an ad hoc working group*, Cabinet Office, London.

Yllo, K. and Bograd, M. (eds) (1988) *Feminist perspectives on wife abuse*, London: Sage.

Acts of Parliament

1976	Domestic Violence and Matrimonial Proceedings Act
1977	Housing (Homeless Persons) Act
1978	Domestic Proceedings and Magistrates Court Act
1989	Children Act
1996	Family Law Act
1996	Housing Act

Appendix A

Methodology

The research was conducted in two stages:

1. A mapping study of inter-agency domestic violence initiatives in England, Scotland and Wales was conducted.

2. This was followed by an in-depth study of three local areas, and policy and practice profile studies in a further five areas, supplemented by secondary research with other domestic violence forums.

Detailed methods used: the mapping study

1. The mapping study was carried out over an eight-month period. A national telephone survey was conducted of all local authorities in Scotland, Wales and England. Initial contacts were made with each authority through the housing department or the local police force. These contacts led to networking and further contacts. Additional interviews were carried out by telephone, as appropriate. The interview topic guide used was piloted with two authorities. It covered general issues involved in inter-agency work on domestic violence, including whether or not such work had been initiated at all, and any plans for future development. Where an initiative was in place, the topic guides included questions on the setting up of the project, membership, the lead agency if appropriate, structure, employment of any workers, participation of Women's Aid and refuge groups, work done, any problems encountered, and so on. Due to the large variety of situations investigated,

interviews were often of an informal nature and were adapted to local circumstances.

2. Refuge groups were also contacted throughout England using written questionnaires requesting information on local inter-agency groupings. The distribution of the questionnaires was facilitated through contributions to the national conference of WAFE, the Women's Aid Federation (England), and through national newsletters. An excellent response rate was achieved.

3. The information gained was updated at the end of the project and put on to a database, sponsored by the Joseph Rowntree Foundation and WAFE, to provide basic information on inter-agency initiatives and domestic violence forums nationally.

The field work in selected areas

1. The detailed fieldwork in selected areas was conducted over a one-year period. The study areas were selected according to a complex set of criteria and after taking advice from a wide variety of domestic violence experts and practitioners, including the Women's Aid federations. The data collected during the mapping study was used as the basis of the selection. The criteria used included:

■ geographical spread;

■ demographic differences;

■ existence of varied multi-racial populations;

- mix of city, small town and rural areas;

- nature of the local authority;

- nature of the inter-agency work done;

- length of time the project had operated;

- stage of development;

- identity of initiating agency (including at least one police-led initiative);

- structure and management;

- resourcing;

- employment of workers;

- role and involvement of Women's Aid and other refuges;

- commitment to equal opportunities;

- involvement of women and children experiencing domestic violence.

2. Similar criteria were applied to the choice of policy and practice profile study areas as to the choice of main study areas. They were selected to represent a wider range of situations in terms of geographical location, urban and rural mix including London, demographic diversity, type of inter-agency work in progress, existence of local refuges, stage reached in the work, and the development of both county level and local level groups.

3. The three localities which were selected as main study areas for the research project were Derby, Walsall and Cleveland.

The five policy and practice profile study areas selected were South Yorkshire, North Wales, Bristol, the London Borough of Greenwich and Dorset.

The main study areas: research conducted

1. In the main study areas, initial meetings were held between the research team and representatives of the three domestic violence inter-agency projects, DDVAG, the Cleveland Domestic Violence Multi-

agency Forum, and the Walsall Domestic Violence Forum. The team then officially approached each forum and asked permission to conduct the study. A variety of meetings to discuss the research study were held, and the researchers attended full domestic violence forum meetings in each area. Formal agreements were reached that the projects would participate in the study and would work actively and closely with the research team.

2. In-depth interviews were held with key members, officers and employees of the domestic violence inter-agency forums in the three main study areas. For some interviewees who were particularly active and involved (eg, employed coordinators and forum chairs), between two and four interviews were conducted. The interview schedule used was piloted in one local authority area. It covered a wide range of issues relating to inter-agency work, including issues addressed in the mapping study which were explored in more detail. It also included investigation of the history and detailed development of the project; policy and practice developments in involved agencies; the conduct of meetings and work undertaken; details of structure, management and employment; the content of equal opportunities work and of strategies to involve Women's Aid, the refuge movement and abused women and children; and plans and ideas for the future of inter-agency work, both locally and nationally.

3. Similarly in-depth interviews were held with representatives of a wide variety of local agencies. Staff were interviewed in local refuges and Women's Aid groups, including specialist refuges for black women and women from minority ethnic communities. Representatives of the local police force were interviewed at both policy-making and practitioner level, and included domestic violence officers and officers in domestic violence units, where these existed. In Cleveland, the deputy Chief Constable of Cleveland Constabulary was interviewed. Representatives were

also interviewed from local authority special units (eg, equalities units); from social services departments and from housing departments; from the probation service; from Victim Support; and from a wide variety of voluntary sector and community agencies. In all, 70 interviews of this type were conducted.

4. Postal questionnaires were also sent to organisations, or sections of organisations, not otherwise contacted to ascertain if they had either knowledge of, or contact with the inter-agency forums in their areas. While it is usually the case that postal surveys elicit a poor return rate, the response to these questionnaires was moderately successful, at least in two of the study areas. Organisations responding included various sections of local statutory agencies which had not been contacted otherwise, and a variety of voluntary organisations which did not have domestic violence as one of their main briefs. A shorter interview schedule was designed for the postal questionnaire to facilitate ease of response.

5. A wide variety of other organisations were contacted for interview by telephone in each research area.

6. A variety of meetings were attended in an observer role in each area. These included full forum meetings, management or steering committee meetings, where relevant, multi-agency training sessions and women's support groups.

7. Documentation, policies, practice guidance and minutes of meetings were collected. These included terms of reference, aims and objectives, equal opportunities policies, mission statements, job descriptions, meeting minutes, mailing lists, leaflets, booklets, posters, and policy and practice guidelines and other material produced by the forum for the public or for local agencies.

8. Seventy women who had experienced domestic violence were interviewed. The research team attempted to build a varied sample, which included both women who had used refuges and who had not; women currently living both in temporary accommodation of various types, including refuges, and in permanent accommodation; women who had experienced different types of violence; black women and women from minority ethnic communities; disabled women; lesbians; women both with children and without; women who had experienced violence from other perpetrators apart from partners; and women who had differential levels of involvement with a variety of agencies.

9. While it was hard to meet all these criteria in each study area, a reasonably varied sample of women was constructed. This was achieved with considerable help from local refuges and other agencies and from forum employees where these existed.

10. Black women and women from minority ethnic communities were offered the choice of being interviewed by a women from a similar racial or ethnic heritage or in their first language (if this was not English) if they wished. However, due to the short length of the interview schedule and its generally non-contentious content, few women took up this option. (This is in marked contrast to the response received in relation to other pieces of research conducted by the research team in which long, complex interviews have been held, sometimes directly addressing issues of racism and other types of discrimination. In these interviews, the majority of women respondents have taken up options for choice of interviewer.)

11. The research team also agreed to offer disabled women the option of being interviewed by a disabled interviewer, and to extend this type of option to other areas of equalities practice, where possible. This development in research methodology as regards issues of equality and anti-discriminatory practice will be applied in other research projects conducted by the team in the future whenever it is possible

to do so. The team is particularly grateful to interviewees in Derby who raised this issue and who assisted in addressing it.

12. Interviews with women were conducted in a supportive, open-ended manner, as is standard practice within the Domestic Violence Research Group as a whole. Confidentiality was ensured, and women were offered the choice of receiving a copy of their interview for amendment and editing, or to keep for future reference, if they so wished. They were also offered the opportunity to stay in touch with the project and to be further involved in the research if they chose to be.

13. Interviews were transcribed and were analysed using a range of research analysis methods. While most of the analysis was qualitative in nature due to the wide variety of issues covered and the diversity and complexity of the data collected, some quantitative analysis was applied to the interview data set collected from women survivors of domestic violence.

The policy and practice profile study areas: research conducted

1. Permission was sought to conduct research in the five policy and practice profile study areas, and a variety of preparatory meetings were held with the local forums and with key personnel.

2. The research conducted in the policy and profile study areas was similar to that conducted in the main study areas except that women who had experienced domestic violence were not interviewed. Key agencies were contacted and interviewed, where possible, using the general agency interview schedule. In general, fewer interviews were conducted in each locality, with 32 interviews in all taking place.

3. Some agencies were approached by telephone and full telephone interviews

were conducted in certain cases. Other local agencies were contacted using the postal questionnaire.

4. Where possible, researchers attended local domestic violence forum meetings, conferences etc. Documentation was collected as in the main study.

5. The data collected was analysed using a variety of qualitative analysis methods as for the main study.

Additional research and dissemination

1. Contacts were made throughout the country with a wide variety of domestic violence forums and projects, involved agencies, local authority specialist units (eg, women's equality units and community safety units), refuges, domestic violence practitioners and other organisations, including, for example, Southall Black Sisters and the national Women's Aid federations. Telephone and face-to-face interviews were conducted where possible. The researchers attended a variety of domestic violence forum meetings in different localities, and both attended, and participated in, relevant conferences, seminars and workshops.

2. Face-to-face interviews were conducted with participants in some of the most established inter-agency domestic violence projects. These included members and employees of the inter-agency forums in Leeds, Nottingham, Hammersmith and Fulham, and Islington. Relevant refuge groups and specialist domestic violence projects (eg, the *Domestic Violence Matters* project in Islington) were also interviewed. Literature and material produced by these projects was collected and studied.

The research findings were disseminated as described in Chapter 3.

Appendix B

Examples of inter-agency documents and terms of reference

This Appendix contains some excerpts from the *terms of reference* of a number of domestic violence forums, not all of which were included among the study areas. Each contains similar sections, only a few of which are included here.

Guiding principles and aims and objectives

This section contains some examples of *guiding principles* and of *aims and objectives* of a number of domestic violence forums.

Excerpt from Principles document, Hammersmith and Fulham Domestic Violence Forum

a) Accepting that domestic violence is a crime and is unacceptable in our community.

b) The services available to a woman should be offered in a non-judgemental way and should aim to maximise her choices.

c) Mutual respect, trust, professionalism and a desire for sensitive and appropriate service delivery are essential to our collaboration.

d) Respect for the accountability of each agency's representatives to their own management/group.

Equal opportunities

a) The Forum, its work and service delivery, will ensure that equal opportunities are incorporated at all stages, and will not discriminate on the basis of colour, race, gender, nationality, sexual preference, marital status, age, class, dis/ability, religious or political beliefs.

b) The Forum recognises that black agencies/people are under-represented in the Forum. The Forum will encourage and seek the participation and involvement of black agencies/people through positive action and by the formation of anti-racist strategies and active recruitment of black members to the Forum.

c) The Forum will also encourage and seek the participation and involvement of other groups and people who may experience discrimination on those grounds outlined in para 2.1.

Aims

To continue developing and implementing an inter-agency strategy on domestic violence which seeks:

a) To promote and maintain cooperation and joint action.

b) To increase awareness of domestic violence in the community and agencies.

c) To improve services and responses to women and children who have experienced or are experiencing domestic violence.

d) To take positive action against perpetrators.

e) To maximise the resources available to promote the above.

(These *aims* are followed by *objectives* and other *terms of reference*.)

Excerpt from Guiding Principles, Hounslow Domestic Violence Forum

1. That the Forum focuses on abuse and violence against women in a broadly domestic situation.

2. That the Forum follows the principles of Equalities, addressing the needs of older women, black and ethnic minority women, disabled women, lesbians and all women who face discrimination.

3. That the Forum is inter-agency and includes all interested parties which accept the guiding principles of the Forum. Participants will respect different ways of working even if not in agreement.

4. That although the main focus of the work is interagency, the Forum will recognise and welcome the contribution survivors can make.

Objectives

1. To increase knowledge and awareness within agencies of domestic violence.

2. To provide opportunities for interaction between agencies including the voluntary sector, and build trust and cooperation between agencies.

3. To influence agencies to improve, promote and coordinate their services to women experiencing domestic violence.

4. To provide information to people affected by domestic violence.

5. To research the needs of women in order to identify gaps in services.

6. To inform and educate the wider community on domestic violence issues and campaign where appropriate.

7. To review the work and terms of reference of the Forum on a regular basis.

Excerpt from terms of reference, South Yorkshire Domestic Violence Multi-agency Working Group

1. To function as a Forum for information exchange between agencies in order to provide victims of domestic violence with the necessary advice and support.

2. To coordinate county-wide initiatives and ad hoc projects.

3. To encourage agencies to develop a code of practice for dealing with domestic violence in South Yorkshire (which respects area policy on responding to domestic violence).

4. To maintain an active and productive approach to multi-agency working.

5. To support and maintain the autonomy of local groups and facilitate local initiatives.

Aims and objectives

1. To raise the awareness and profile of domestic violence in South Yorkshire.

2. To identify and pool resource needs and raise finance for county-wide initiatives.

3. To promote multi-agency training in South Yorkshire.

4. To respond to a local, national and international agenda on domestic violence and develop links with other projects.

5. To identify differences between areas in their response to domestic violence by sharing and exchanging information, in order to influence the delivery of quality services in South Yorkshire.

Excerpt from Aims and objectives, Dorset Inter-agency Forum for Domestic Violence

The *aim* of the inter-agency strategy is to achieve inter-agency cooperation and awareness in order to establish agreed: policy, procedure, practice guidance, information to the public.

The *objectives* to be achieved are:

1. *Support*: to further promote the development of information and support services for victims/survivors of domestic and family violence.

2. *Child protection*: to develop multi-agency procedures which highlight the connection between family violence and risk of physical abuse; effects of marital/family violence and emotional consequences; recognition of the concealment of violence, within the family or directed towards children, and reduce the risks to those children affected.

3. *Criminal Justice*: to determine the response to the commission of offences to include: the tariff of arrest and charges brought in relation to a particular offence and the management of offenders within the criminal justice system.

4. *Treatment*: to develop systems towards support and management of perpetrators of domestic violence.

5. *Information*: to produce a 'directory' of local information and resources.

6. *Education*: to promote opportunities for raising public and professional awareness of the issues and relevant networks available.

7. *Training*: to promote the inclusion of domestic and family violence knowledge and awareness in multi-agency and individual agency training programmes.

Further terms of reference

Substantial extracts from the *terms of reference* of the domestic violence forum in one of the main research areas are included as an illustration. It is not possible to include examples from all of the study areas of *terms of reference* gathered during the course of the research.

Principles and mission statement, Derby Domestic Violence Action Group, DDVAG

1. Domestic violence is defined by the Forum as:

> ... the emotional, physical, sexual or psychological abuse of a person by their partner, family member or someone with whom there is, or has been, a relationship.

2. Members of this Forum accept that domestic violence is a serious crime which is unacceptable to society, and that all individuals have a right to live their lives free of abuse and/or the threat of violence.

3. The Forum has adopted a holistic approach to the prevention of domestic violence which involves increasing the availability of protection and support offered to survivors as well as access to help for perpetrators.

4. The Forum acknowledges that domestic violence essentially involves the misuse of power and the exercise of control by one person, usually a man, over another, usually a woman. The two are, or have been, in some intimate relationship with each other.

5. The work of the Forum is informed by the experiences of survivors of domestic violence which indicate it involves a range of different types of abuse which may include severe physical assault, rape and sexual abuse, and mental/emotional abuse involving degradation, humiliation, verbal abuse, threats and withholding money.

6. Any women or child can be abused, irrespective of race, class, age, religion, sexuality, mental or physical ability.

7. Members of the Forum also acknowledge there are many reasons why women stay in abusive relationships which

may include fear, love, financial dependency, isolation, religion, or children. No one deserves to be abused. Often a woman wants the violence to stop but not the relationship to end. The personal relationship between the abused person and the perpetrator of the violence must always be considered.

8. The Forum recognises that the non-judgemental models of working with domestic violence developed by the women's voluntary sector (eg, Women's Aid, Hadhari Nari and Rape Crisis) are crucial in helping to meet the needs of abused women and their children.

9. Members of the Forum accept that:

> Domestic violence requires an interagency response involving co-ordination and collaboration of a range of social, legal, financial and health resources. This Forum aims to work towards the development of a common policy and best practice to enable and empower people to live their lives free of violence

It is the intention of DDVAG to bring about social, institutional and community change with regard to domestic violence. Our mission statement is as follows:

> To achieve the general acceptance that domestic violence is a crime and unacceptable to society, to ensure that support is given to people experiencing domestic violence and help for perpetrators is readily available and accessible.

Equal opportunities policy, DDVAG

DDVAG is committed to equal opportunities and treatment for all regardless of gender, race, colour, ethnic or national origin, religion, disability, age, appearance, marital status or sexuality. We recognise that many groups are disadvantaged in our society and we will seek to actively assist disadvantaged groups to participate in our work and benefit from our services.

Membership: membership of DDVAG and the Forum is open to representatives from any interested group. All members are expected to uphold group policy, and no member will be treated less favourably than other persons because of their gender, race, colour, ethnic or national origin, religion, disability, age, appearance, marital status or sexuality. We will actively seek to ensure that disadvantaged minority groups are represented on DDVAG.

Targeting services: DDVAG recognises that in the vast majority of cases, it is women who are the victims of domestic violence from known men. We also acknowledge that women are a disadvantaged group who have less income, housing, transport and other services. We therefore choose to target our services specifically at women. We acknowledge that men too experience domestic violence, and endeavour to support services for men provided these do not in any way diminish service provision for women, eg, by competing for scarce resources.

DDVAG will actively assist dis-advantaged minority groups to benefit from its services. We will seek to identify the needs of minority groups, especially black and disabled women, and establish close relationships with these groups. We will collect and monitor records of those who use services for victims of domestic violence and take steps to improve accessibility of services to disadvantaged groups who are under-represented.

Employment: as an employer DDVAG will ensure that no job applicant or employee receives less favourable treatment on the grounds of gender, race, colour, ethnic or national origin, religion, disability, age, appearance, marital status or sexuality (except where allowed under the law and is necessary). In addition, we will seek actively to encourage applications from minority groups in order to achieve equality of opportunity. Interview and appointment procedures shall be adopted so as to minimise any disadvantage suffered by any minority group.

Appendix C

Useful addresses

The 1995 Home Office inter-agency circular, *Inter-agency coordination to tackle domestic violence*, is available from:

Action against Crime Unit
Home Office, 50 Queen Anne's Gate, London SW1H 0AT, Tel 0171 273 2625

WAFE, The Women's Aid Federation (England)
PO Box 391, Bristol BS99 7WS, Tel 0117 944 4411
WAFE National Helpline, Tel 0117 963 3542

Welsh Women's Aid
Cardiff Office, 38-48 Crwys Road, Cardiff, Wales CF2 4NN, Tel 01222 390874
Aberystwyth Office, 4 Pound Place, Aberystwyth, Wales, Tel 01970 612748
Rhyl Office, 26 Wellington Street, Rhyl, Wales LL18 1BN, Tel 01745 334767

Scottish Women's Aid
12 Torphichen Street, Edinburgh, Scotland EH3 8JQ, Tel 0131 221 0401

Northern Ireland Women's Aid
129 University Street, Belfast, Northern Ireland BT7 1HP, Tel 01232 249041
Women's Aid Helpline in Northern Ireland, Tel 01232 331818